LAW

AND

PUPIL CONTROL

BY

ANNE FLOWERS

Associate Professor of Education
Columbia College,
Columbia, South Carolina

AND

EDWARD C. BOLMEIER

Professor of Education
Duke University
Durham, North Carolina

AMERICAN SCHOOL LAW SERIES

CINCINNATI

THE W. H. ANDERSON COMPANY

FOREWORD

The administration of the pupil personnel in our public schools gives rise to many important practical problems. These problems involve all concerned with the schools— pupils, teachers, administrators, parents— and the effectiveness of the whole school program may very well be influenced by the way they are met.

State legislatures may and often do enact statutes governing one aspect or another of the rights and duties of school children and their parents. In the main, however, they leave such matters to the discretion of local school boards. When parents are dissatisfied with the policies and regulations of a board, they may appeal to the courts to protect what they may regard as their rights and the rights of their children. In deciding cases of this kind, the courts have formulated broad general principles to be applied by the school board in dealing with pupils.

The rule is well established that, in the absence of specific statutory authority or limitation, a board of education may enforce any rule or regulation that is reasonably necessary to protect the best interests of the school. The courts are very reluctant to declare a board regulation unreasonable. They will never substitute their own discretion for that of the school authorities; the enforcement of a rule will never be enjoined because, in the opinion of the court, it is unwise or inexpedient; a rule will not be set aside unless it appears to be unreasonable.

Broad legal principles such as those just stated are necessary but their full meaning is seen only when they are applied to specific situations and problems. The authors of this book have selected a number of important aspects of pupil control and they have made an exhaustive study of the court decisions governing them. Certain characteristics of the book are noteworthy: (1) it deals with very practical problems, (2) the treatment of the law governing these problems is exhaustive, (3) the writing is clear and precise. The book is a substantial contribution to the growing body of school law and it should have wide use.

NEWTON EDWARDS
Professor Emeritus
University of Chicago

AMERICAN SCHOOL LAW SERIES

ADVISORY EDITORS

ROBERT L. DRURY
of the Ohio Bar

LEGAL COUNSEL, OHIO EDUCATION ASSOCIATION

Author: Drury's Ohio School Guide;
Editor: Law and the School Superintendent

EDWARD C. BOLMEIER

PROFESSOR OF EDUCATION, DUKE UNIVERSITY

Co-Author: Law and Pupil Control;
Courts and the Curriculum

CONTENTS

vii

Chapter 1

INTRODUCTION

Teachers, school officials, and legislators all realize the necessity for adequate pupil control in order to accomplish the purposes for which the schools exist. Without school control anarchy and pandemonium would reign and the schools would be ineffective to say the least.

The courts also recognize the need for proper legal control as is evidenced by the many decisions upholding litigated rules and regulations governing pupil control, which are reasonable and within the framework of the constitutions and the statutes. The court decisions serve as precedents for consideration of subsequent cases. These judicial precedents constitute legal principles which should aid the school administrator and teacher in dealing with the problem of pupil control.

§ 1.1 Allocation of authority and responsibility

Within constitutional limits, state legislatures have plenary authority with respect to matters of policy for school control. Statutes, however, are usually rather general in matters dealing with the control of pupils. Actually much of the legislation concerning school control is permissive in nature, thereby delegating to school districts the authority and responsibility to legislate the specifics of school control. This is considered proper in view of the fact that a school district is merely a territorial subdivision of the state, and as such the school board members are state officials performing the state function of education. The school board may be thought of as a legislative body enacting rules and regulations governing school control within the boundaries of the school district. The board rules and regulations may be considered legal if they pass the test of reasonableness and constitutionality.

1

The delegating process does not necessarily terminate at the steps of school boards. The local school board, which has general charge and superintendence of the public schools, delegates authority and responsibility to school personnel for exercising the necessary control over pupils.

Moreover, by virtue of their professional positions, school personnel have authority and responsibility which even school boards do not possess. "The law does not contemplate that the members of a board of education shall supervise the professional work of teachers, principals, and superintendents. They are not teachers, and ordinarily, not qualified to be such. Generally they do not possess qualifications to pass upon methods of instruction and discipline. The law clearly contemplates that the professionally trained teachers, principals, and superintendents shall have exclusive control of these matters."[1]

The classroom teacher has a closer association with, and understanding of, the pupil than do other school personnel; thereby possessing a special legal relationship. In fact, one of the basic legal principles regarding pupil control is that the teacher, by virtue of his position, has legal authority over a pupil analogous to that which a parent has over his child, at least for purposes of necessary control, restraint, and correction.

Very frequently the aspirations or actions of pupils collide with statutory provisions or with the rules and regulations of school officials, administrators, and teachers. It is only natural that pupils sometimes object to certain restrictions and requirements imposed upon them, even though those responsible for making them consider them desirable and necessary for the proper conduct and morale of the school. When the restrictions and requirements appear to be unnecessary, unreasonable, and illegal, a pupil, or his parent, is privileged to stand up for his legal rights.

Obviously there may be a lack of agreement among the various parties concerned as to what is necessary, reasonable, and legal for maintaining school control. When

---

[1] State v. Board of Education of Lewis County, 125 WVa 579, 25 SE (2d) 537 (1943).

the disagreement reaches the stage of litigation, the courts determine the legality of the rules and regulations upon which there is disagreement. Ultimately then, final authority rests with the courts.

§ 1.2 Reasonableness as a determinant of legality

As in so many litigating circumstances of school matters, the courts invariably apply the test of reasonableness in determining whether or not school officers, administrators, or teachers have exceeded their legal authority in formulating or enforcing certain rules and regulations governing the control of pupils.

Unfortunately the courts are frequently criticized for inconsistency and vacillation merely because a court decision concerning reasonableness of pupil control may be in favor of the plaintiff in one case and in favor of the defendant in another case where, on the surface, the two cases appear to be similar.

Accusations of judicial inconsistencies regarding pupil control are too often due to ignorance of the circumstances of each particular case. Illustrations abound in virtually all areas of school law cases. Consider for example from the two following cases what is "reasonable" in administering corporal punishment for misconduct.

In a Texas case[2] a court upheld a teacher for forcefully using a big club on a pupil. (But the facts of the case show that the pupil was over seventeen years of age and larger in size and weight than the teacher and that he came to school armed with a pistol and threatened to shoot the teacher when he asked for the gun.)

In a similar case as far as allegations are concerned but a dissimilar one as far as circumstances are concerned,[3] a court held a teacher liable merely for sitting on a pupil in order to subdue him during a fit of anger. (But the facts of this case show that the pupil was only ten years old and weighed less than ninety pounds, whereas, the teacher

---

[2] Metcalf v. State, 21 TexApp 174, 17 SW 142 (1886).
[3] Calway v. Williamson, 130 Conn 575, 36 A(2d) 377 (1944).

who infuriated the child was a big husky scrapper weighing
approximately 200 pounds.)

Although "reasonableness" is a question of law to be
determined by the courts, they are usually reluctant to pass
upon the "wisdom" or "unwisdom" of school policies and
practices. Despite accusations to the contrary, courts do
not attempt to legislate for the public schools. Their
responsibility is to interpret the laws, rules, and regulations
with respect to constitutionality, legislative intent, and
reasonableness.

§ 1.3 Main areas of current concern

Innumerable situations exist in the public schools where
certain types of pupil control are considered to be desirable
and necessary by some but undesirable and unnecessary
by others. Virtually all of them are controversial and
fraught with potential litigation. Those broad areas in
which the litigious aspects of pupil control are more timely
and significant are indicated by the chapter headings of
this publication.

The main purpose of this book is to report judicial decisions of the higher courts (appellate courts of the various
states and of the United States) which furnish some insight
into the legal aspects of pupil control. Categorically, the
broad areas to be treated relate to legal aspects of such
problems as: (1) membership in secret societies, (2) rules
and regulations concerning married pupils, (3) regulations
of dress and appearance of pupils, (4) rules and regulations pertaining to health, and (5) willful misconduct of
pupils.

The legality of methods employed in enforcing pupil
control is also significant and of timely concern. It is not,
however, treated in a separate chapter due to the fact
that it is frequently referred to throughout the book where
it is applicable to the incidents of pupil activity discussed in
the various chapters.

(a) Secret societies. Secret societies, such as fraternities
and sororities, in the public high schools were most prevalent several decades ago. In the opinion of school officials

and administrators, these organizations were detrimental to the welfare and morale of the student body. Consequently several states enacted legislation designed to prohibit the perpetuation of the secret societies. Many school systems merely formulated rules and regulations barring the organization under the general legislation which permits them to exercise discretionary authority to adopt measures to maintain proper control over the schools.

In order to implement the rules and regulations against the secret societies, restrictions were imposed which prohibited members from participating in certain school activities. Obviously strenuous objections arose on the part of pupils and parents—sometimes to the point of litigation. As will be pointed out in the following chapter, the courts have been quite consistent in upholding the legality of the school board's rules.

It is noteworthy that the number of court cases pertaining to this problem is waning. This may be due, in part, to the fact that by now the legal principle outlawing the secret societies is so firmly established that its reversal is considered unlikely. If, however, the prediction that the forced integration of public schools may cause the secret societies to flourish again becomes true, the pendulum may swing back and a rash of court cases on the problem may be triggered again.

(b) Married pupils. In contrast with the declining litigation concerning secret societies, court cases pertaining to the problem of high school marriages are on the upswing. More than half of all the higher court cases involving high school marriages have occurred since 1957.

The legal principle growing out of the two earliest cases was so convincingly established that there are likely to be no more cases in which the married pupils' right to attend school will be contested. Moreover, two later cases where married girls were relieved from complying with school attendance regulations have likely marked the end of litigation on that score.

The court cases on the marriage problem which are most significant and recent are those which grow out of regulations which penalize married high school boys who marry. The most common type of a penalty here is where the married boy is prohibited from participating in athletic activities. Although the courts have generally upheld the legality of these restrictive measures, careful reading, particularly in the courts' dicta, will reveal some reservation on the part of judges as to the wisdom of the school boards' policies.

Litigation on this problem is likely to accelerate and to become more complex. The mere fact that there is a growing tendency for marriages to occur at earlier ages throughout the nation is likely to augment the school's difficulty in curbing marriages.

It will be interesting to see where schools which are adding the thirteenth and fourteenth grades to their systems will have the "cut-off," if any, as to where marriages will be condoned.

(c) Dress and appearance of pupils. At first blush it might appear that the school board's regulations regarding such matters as pupils' attire, and the litigation caused thereby, are trivial and inconsequential. A careful analysis of the problem, however, will indicate otherwise.

The outlandish and ridiculous dress of boys and girls in this beatnik age is largely a manifestation of youth's rebellion to conformance and regulation. It seems that when rules and regulations prescribe what must or must not be worn in school, the desire on the part of youth to rebel is kindled. Of course, when the school's prescribed rules are violated it becomes necessary for the school authorities to enforce them; otherwise, disobedience to law would be encouraged in other situations.

Since most parents believe that the manner in which their children dress is a matter for them to decide, it is only natural that they should resent the school's usurpation of this prerogative. The resentment frequently results in defiance, and the defiance develops into actual litigation. Fortunately most cases involving the controversies over regulations of pupils' dress are settled in the principal's office or in the lower courts. Only those cases which reach the higher courts are discussed in chapter 4 of this publication.

(d) Health of pupils. Over the past century there has been a steady increase in the school's assumption for the responsibility of promoting and safeguarding the pupils' mental and physical health. Of all phases of health measures for pupils which have been adjudicated, that of vaccination is predominant.

As will be indicated in chapter 5, the courts' decisions on vaccination controversies have varied because of the different circumstances surrounding individual cases. From time to time there have been disputed opinions as to the harm or benefit derived from vaccination. Apparently the courts have not yet settled the issue for all possible cases.

Considering the current practice of innoculating pupils for communicable diseases, other than smallpox, it is surprising that more litigation has not yet developed. Perhaps it is due to the fact that these innoculations are usually less mandatory than are vaccinations for smallpox.

Since increased attention is being given in the public schools for individual differences, there is likely to be more litigation regarding this matter. So far most of it has had to do with objections to the school's method of classification of pupils for whom special attention is provided.

(e) Willful misconduct of pupils. The willful misconduct of pupils constitutes one of the most serious and vexing problems of pupil control with which school officials and teachers must cope. To overlook premeditated misbehavior could be detrimental to the future development of the pupil and injurious to the morale and government of the school. To invoke punitive measures is considered by some to be merely a temporary expedient and not a suitable deterrent. Although the latter is the more common practice, it is also the more vulnerable to litigation.

One of the most serious aspects of pupil misconduct has to do with the deliberate destruction or defacement of school property. Under the common law, until recently, the legal principle prevailed that neither a minor child nor his parent is financially responsible for the acts of a child. The growing belief now, however, is that parents should assume legal responsibility (liability) for the damaging acts of their children. Consequently several states have enacted (judicially approved) legislation designed to hold parents financially liable for damages caused to school property by their children.

A New Jersey case, referred to in chapter 6, in which more than a third of a million dollars damage was caused by the willful destruction of a school building by a boy, indicates the potential immensity of the liability for this type of pupil misconduct.

§ 1.4 Legality of methods employed in enforcing pupil control

Rules and regulations for pupil control are not usually contested in the courts. It is the methods employed in the enforcement of the rules and regulations which frequently cause the actual litigation. Of course school board rules and regulations ordinarily are accompanied by stipulated consequences if they are violated.

Various methods of enforcing pupil control are referred to in this publication as they apply to the incidents in court cases reviewed. The order of importance of the different methods employed is a matter of personal judgment. On the basis of the number of court cases and amount of literature on the subject, corporal punishment would likely top the list in importance, followed in order by expulsion and suspension.

(a) Corporal punishment. Although there have been more court cases in the past concerning corporal punishment for misconduct, it must be admitted that, as a mode of enforcing pupil control, it has lately been less frequently employed than either expulsion or suspension. This may be partially due to the fact that legal principles limiting the degree of physical punishment are so firmly established as to make corporal punishment rather ineffective as a deterrent of pupil misconduct. The legal principles derived from court cases indicate that the corporal punishment,

if administered, should: (1) be in conformance with statutory enactment; (2) be for the purpose of correction without malice; (3) not be cruel or excessive so as to leave permanent marks or injuries; and (4) be suited to the age and sex of the pupil. Essentially, in order for corporal punishment to be legal, it must be reasonable in the eyes of the judiciary.

There is the possibility that the pendulum is about to swing back toward greater "use of the rod" in the public schools. With the alarming state of juvenile delinquency, some persons attribute the cause to the "luke-warm" discipline measures employed in the public schools.

A movement toward harsher policies regarding corporal punishment is discernible throughout the nation. "Milwaukee and San Francisco have taken sterner positions in favor of corporal punishment practices in schools. A third large city, Washington, D. C., is now trying to do the same thing."[4]

In an unusual arrangement of local government where Congress acts as a "city council" for Washington, with authority to pass measures on certain school matters, a bill was approved in 1963 by the House of Representatives to repeal a regulation barring the use of physical punishment in the schools. Even though a majority of the school board opposed the bill on the grounds that teachers already had authority to restrain unruly pupils by leading them out of the classroom, and that further use of force would create more problems than it would solve, the legislators stuck by their "spare-the-rod-and-spoil the child" conviction.

Even though corporal punishment is authorized in Milwaukee and San Francisco, it is noteworthy that "both districts continue to forbid physical punishment after the act has been committed."[5]

(b) Expulsion and suspension. The legal principle is firmly established that school authorities may expel or suspend from school any pupil who disobeys a reasonable rule

---

[4] "Three Cities Move to Toughen Corporal Punishment Policies," Nation's Schools, LXXIII (September, 1963), p. 78.
[5] Ibid.

or regulation. School officials are clothed with considerable discretionary authority in determining whether or not a rule has been violated, and, in the event they conclude that a violation has occurred, they also have discretionary authority in determining the nature of penalty to be imposed—provided it is not arbitrary or unreasonable. When, however, parents challenge the action of school boards or their employes as being beyond the bounds of reasonableness, litigation may develop.

A number of cases are reviewed in following chapters which indicate certain disputed rules and regulations, the violation of which have resulted in suspension or expulsion. It will be noted that the courts invariably base their decisions upon the *reasonableness* of the rules and the penalties for their violation.

The terms "suspension" and "expulsion" are sometimes used interchangeably. There is, however, considerable difference in the legal meaning of the two terms. "Suspension" is generally an act of the professional school staff, whereas, "expulsion" is a prerogative of the school board. Suspension is usually for a short period of time, or until the pupil conforms to the rule or regulation involved, whereas expulsion is usually permanent, or at least for a substantial length of time.

The court, as well as others, frequently looks somewhat askant at acts of suspension, and particularly at expulsion, as reasonable and profitable methods for forcing the pupils' conformance to prescribed rules and regulations. Some incorrigible youngsters violate school regulations for the very purpose of being removed from the school environment. Moreover, when a pupil is denied school attendance he is deprived of education designed for his betterment. Of course when a pupil's misconduct or disobedience is of such a grave nature that his presence is disrupting to the school and detrimental to the morale of the student body, suspension or even expulsion, is likely to be judicially condoned.

Chapter 2

AUTHORITY OF SCHOOL OFFICIALS TO RESTRICT MEMBERSHIP OF PUPILS IN SECRET SOCIETIES

Faced with the realization that so-called secret societies were not another of the fads often adopted by teenagers but rather an association of pupils which brought to the school and its personnel complaints from irate or disappointed parents whose children were not accepted for membership; undesirable influences which were evident in school elections, social affairs, extracurricular activities, and school spirit; and embarrassment and criticism for activities such as weekend trips, dances, and beach parties that did not have the sanction of the school but claimed the name of the school, administrators and other interested citizens throughout the country have made attempts to remedy the situation by requesting boards of education to adopt rules and regulations which prohibit pupil membership in such societies.

Secret societies, which seem to have at least one element in common, that of selectivity of membership, made their appearance early in the educational institutions of America with the founding of Phi Beta Kappa, the first fraternity, at the College of William and Mary in 1776; but not until one hundred years had elapsed was Alpha Pi, a literary society and the first Greek-letter society in the public high school, founded.[1]

Secret societies, often called sororities, fraternities, or Greek-letter societies, enjoyed increased popularity as high school pupils attempted to mimic their counterparts in college; and the last decade of the nineteenth century is

---

[1] Thomas Gates, "Passage of the California Anti-Fraternity Statute," California Journal of Secondary Education, XXX (February, 1955), p. 83.

often cited as the period in which secret societies became well-known as a part of high school life in many areas of the country. Without denying the commendable purposes for which many of these societies were formed, many educators have gone on record as being opposed to secret societies; and as a result of the increasing concern expressed by their constituents, the legislators of at least half of the states have enacted statutes which prohibit membership in secret societies by those enrolled in the public schools or which provide specific authority to local school officials to adopt rules of a regulatory nature concerning organizations which are considered detrimental to the welfare of the school.[2]

§ 2.1 Secret societies, a nationwide problem

Although pressure from the public has produced legislative enactments dealing with the legality of high school fraternities and sororities, actual elimination of these societies has been difficult; and actions taken by school authorities have been targets for litigation. The belief that restriction of membership in secret societies is an invasion of parental authority coupled with the lack of support by parents and community leaders in attempts to abolish secret societies, the lack of recognition or admittance by school officials of the existence of societies, the lack of initiative on the part of school authorities or parents in eliminating societies, and the lack of interest and cooperation from young people in destroying an organization in which they hold membership has contributed to secret societies' becoming a nationwide problem in high schools.[3]

For all ages, the most forceful drive is the drive for prestige and power connected with a social organization, but at no time is it so strong as at adolescence, when physical change makes it very necessary for the individual

---

[2] Louise Cooper, "The Legality and Propriety of Secret Societies in High School," (unpublished Master's thesis, Department of Education, Duke University, 1960), p. 63.

[3] John Milligan and Charles Snover, "High School Secret Societies: A Nationwide Problem," American School Board Journal, CXV (August, 1947), pp. 26 to 28.

to have emotional security and status in the eyes of others. It is at this time that the child loses interest in adult-sponsored activities such as Boy Scouts and church groups, and seeks the smaller, more homogeneous intimate group. If the group has an aura of mystery and glamour, and it is known that only the "best group" belong, he will do everything in his power to become one of that group. Membership may assume an importance which seems out of all proportion to an adult, but to the adolescent, well, if he can't get in, he "might as well be dead."[4]

The closed meetings, exclusiveness, social affairs, initiations, and insignia of fraternities and sororities provide young people with many experiences usually reserved for adults. Arguments presented in behalf of high school secret societies include: they have worthy purposes and high ideals; they encourage members to participate actively in school affairs; they aid in developing good scholarship, leadership, and organizational ability; they encourage respect for authority; they provide opportunities for heterosexual social activities; and they keep some pupils in school who might otherwise drop out.[5]

In 1904, Morrison in his address to the members attending the forty-third annual meeting of the National Educational Association reported the findings of a letter sent to 200 principals requesting their feelings toward secret fraternities in the high school.[6] Of the 185 responses only four did not express disapproval. Morrison states:

The consensus of opinion, so far as I can gather it, seems to be: (1) that they are unnecessary in a school where they are at home and under the guardianship of their

---

[4] Virginia Hamilton, "Secret Societies in American High Schools," The Bulletin of The National Association of Secondary-School Principals, XL (October, 1956), p. 22. Reprinted by permission, copyright: Washington, D.C.

[5] Ibid., p. 24.

[6] Gilbert Morrison, "Secret Fraternities in High Schools," Journal of Proceedings and Addresses of The Forty-Third Annual Meeting of The National Educational Association (June, 1904), pp. 484 to 490.

parents, as in the case with high-school children; (2) that whatever good that might be claimed for college fraternities could not apply to boys of high-school age whose character and judgments are unformed; (3) that schools supported by all the people should be democratic and free from caste and organized snobbery; (4) that the fraternities among children of high-school age do have a tendency to set up social exclusiveness and caste in the school; (5) that they are a source of discord among the pupils; (6) that they become factional in their characters and that loyalty to the fraternity generally means disloyalty to everything else; (7) that they dissipate the energies of the pupils and interfere with their studies; (8) that they are selfish and narrow in their aims and methods; (9) that the conduct of pupils should be open and above board, and there is no legitimate want or need in child-nature which calls for secret or dark-lantern proceedings; and (10) that whatever of a social nature which it is necessary to encourage in school can be done thru other and better forms of society which can be under supervision and control of the principal and teachers.[7]

Encouraged by early court decisions and the report made by Morrison, teachers and administrators began to express opinions which were reflected in the resolution submitted and adopted by the National Educational Association in 1905:

. . . The importance to the schools of the first court decisions is so great that it seems to us that nothing should be left undone in propagating the sentiment so strongly prevalent among educators.

Therefore, your committee submits that,

WHEREAS, The sentiment of superintendents, principals, and teachers against secret fraternities is almost universal, and their testimony . . . coincides with the observation and experience of the members of the committee individually, be it therefore,

---

[7] Ibid., p. 488.

Resolved, That we condemn those secret organizations, because they are subversive of the principles of democracy which should prevail in the public schools; because they are selfish, and tend to narrow the minds and sympathies of the pupils; because they stir up strife and contention; because they are snobbish; because they dissipate energy and proper ambition; because they set wrong standards; because rewards are not based on merit, but on fraternity vows; because they inculcate a feeling of self-sufficiency among the members; because secondary-school boys are too young for club life; because they are expensive and foster habits of extravagance; because they bring politics into the legitimate organizations of the school; because they detract interest from study; and because all legitimate elements for good—social, moral, and intellectual—which these societies claim to possess can be better supplied to the pupils through the school at large in the form of literary societies and clubs under the sanction and supervision of the faculties of the school.[8]

With the expression of strong opposition by the official teachers' organization and with the passage of an increasing number of statutes providing a legal basis for the elimination of secret societies, one would anticipate a short-lived existence for the societies in the public high schools. To the contrary, today, a half a century after the adoption of the resolution by the National Education Association condemning secret societies in the public schools, it is not unusual or difficult to locate articles in magazines and newspapers which differ in phraseology only from earlier publications in reporting the behavior of young people in such societies and the problems posed by their presence in the high school.

There are reports of students who are unable to attend school due to injuries sustained in initiations, of parties in downtown hotels, of athletes' refusing to play in competition with non-fraternity athletes, of discrimination in

---

[8] Gilbert Morrison, "Report of The Committee on Secret Fraternities," Journal of Proceedings and Addresses of the Forty-Fourth Annual Meeting of the National Educational Association (July, 1905), p. 451.

selecting members based upon nationality or wealth, and of stealing in order to pay fraternity assessments.[9] Local citizens' committees have requested boards of education to close teenage social clubs when a survey disclosed that ". . . boys' clubs considered drinking 'almost a requirement' and girls' clubs 'find not only drinking, but sexual immorality an acceptable pattern of behavior'."[10]

Former members relate experiences on initiation night: On "Hell Night" he had been taken to a faraway golf course "where the cops can't hear you yell," forced to drink a mixture of searing hot sauce compounded with pepper and garlic, and ordered to smoke a handful of cigars, inhaling every puff. After he vomited, the "hackers" went to work, whacked him 50 times with an inch-thick paddle. "Some of the kids give themselves shots of Novocain, . . . but that just hurts worse when it wears off."[11]

A mother described her son after "Hell Night" as not looking human as his body covered with blood, molasses, and sawdust shook convulsively.[12]

Those who doubt that such activities are present among girls would be enlightened to read the account of an initiation night witnessed by a European visitor to this country:

The high-school girls—there were about 15 of them—were dressed for a tea party, but they carried long bundles containing paddles, and pails for vomiting. In the corner of the room one girl was mixing a drink of castor oil, cold cooking grease, coffee grounds, raw oysters and mackerels' eyes.

The first girl to be initiated was brought in, wearing a bathing suit and a blindfold. She was pale, trembling, and sweating. They made her lie on the floor, face up. Then one girl poured the concoction into her mouth.

---

9 "Gang Busters," Time, LIII (January 17, 1949), p. 46.

10 "Teen-Age Clubs In Greensboro Said Drinking and Sex Centers," The Durham Sun, LXXIV, No. CXCII (October 10, 1962), p. 3-A.

11 "High-School Hell," Time, LIV (October 31, 1949), p. 37.

12 Ibid.

She choked and retched. Two girls held her shoulders. They told her that if she vomited, she would have to drink it back. Some of the castor oil started coming out of her nose. The girls told her: "You goat, you have to drink it all."

Then they made her take a crawling position, and took turns burning her back with lighted cigarettes—not deep, just enough to leave blisters. Meanwhile another girl was throwing an egg at her face. She started to cry and they kicked her. Then they spun her around until she was dizzy and started to vomit, but the girls grabbed hold of her nose and mouth so she couldn't.

. . . Next they told her to assume the angle—kneeling with her head down on her arms, which were flat on the floor. . . . Each girl walked behind her and hit her three times with a paddle, very hard. . . . With every blow she would fall down flat. . . .

After several beatings, she fainted. I thought the others would be frightened then, but they weren't—they seemed angry. They threw cold water in her face. After a few minutes she revived. They made her get into position again. . . .

The next day, I asked my young friend whether she had had any fun last night. "Not exactly," she said, "but it was one of those things that has to be done. You have to, to join a sorority. Otherwise you can't go to dances and everything."[13]

As numerous as the descriptions of experiences of those who are accepted for membership may be, there are found almost as many accounts of the disappointment suffered because of rejection by a desired fraternity or sorority. Letters have been written to school officials relating the disillusionment and unhappiness of a child because he has been unable to pledge the coveted group.[14] Despair in

---

[13] "Secret Ceremony," Time, XLIX (January 13, 1947), p. 80.

[14] Ewing Konold, "How Can the Administrator Deal With Secret Societies in the Secondary School?" The Bulletin of The National Association of Secondary School Principals, XXXIV (March, 1950), p. 279.

some instances has grown to such proportion as to claim the life of its victim.[15]

Many school authorities, charged with the difficult task of decision making, have expressed their belief that it is neither within the power nor is it the responsibility of the school to regulate the activities of youth which occur out of school hours and off the school campus. They and their supporters maintain that any regulatory action concerning membership in fraternities or sororities would be an invasion of parental rights and not in the domain of the school. Others, either because they have felt pressure from the public or because they feel that secret societies are detrimental to the best interests of the school, have enlisted aid from pupils, parents, and other interested individuals in attempting to substitute activities under the supervision and guidance of trained personnel for those activities provided by fraternities and sororities.

Either because their attempts have been unsuccessful or because attempts seem impractical, a number of school officials, claiming their authority from specific statutory provisions or as a part of their general discretionary authority, have felt the necessity to enforce prohibitory rules concerning secret societies. Out of the enforcement of these rules and regulations has come litigation which challenges either the statutory enactment or local regulations as being unreasonable, arbitrary, discriminatory, or unconstitutional.

An examination of appellate court decisions can serve to establish a legal precedent as a guide for those anticipating action related to secret societies.

§ 2.2 Antifraternity rules and regulations supported by specific statutes

In a number of states the legislatures have not deemed it necessary or wise to enact legislation prohibiting membership in secret societies by those enrolled in the public schools, and in a number of states there has been no litigation to challenge the existing statutes or the authority of

---

[15] Hamilton, "Secret Societies in American High Schools," supra, n. 4, p. 23.

boards of education to ban secret societies from the elementary and secondary schools of the state. Without a doubt difficulties and conflicts have arisen in many areas which have not been reported and which have never reached the lower or appellate courts because they have been settled locally in a manner satisfactory to the affected parties. Some instances may be found, however, where courts are asked to enjoin the enforcement of a rule adopted in accordance with a specific state statute, where courts are asked to clarify a statute that exists in terms of constitutionality, and where courts are asked to compel the reinstatement of a pupil who has been suspended or expelled as a result of the enforcement of a rule. It is those instances which furnish insight into the legal authority of school officials to restrict membership of pupils in secret societies.

In 1909, shortly after the suicide of a high-school girl who had had sorority troubles,[16] the state of California enacted a statute which forbade any elementary or secondary school pupil membership or a part in organizing any fraternity, sorority, or secret society which drew its membership partially or entirely from pupils attending the public schools and gave as the exception such organizations as the Native Sons of the Golden West, Native Daughters of the Golden West, Foresters of America or kindred organizations which were not directly associated with the public schools. The statute empowered boards of education to make any local rules or regulations necessary to carry out the enforcement of the act.[17]

The first challenge to the California statute came from San Francisco where Doris Bradford, a pupil in the public high school and a member of a secret society, was suspended from school in compliance with local rules.[18] The judge in rendering the decision of the court recited the history of the growth and expansion of fraternities and sororities and

---

[16] Gates, "Passage of the California Anti-Fraternity Statute," supra, n. 1, p. 85.

[17] Bradford v. Board of Education of City and County of San Francisco, 18 CalApp 19, 121 Pac 929 (1912).

[18] Ibid.

credited another with saying that fraternities and sororities had ". . . become so numerous . . . as to make it necessary to manipulate the Greek alphabet in an artful way in order to make the necessary distinctions." In contrasting the effect of secret societies upon college students and high school students, Justice Kerrigan stated:

> . . . it is quite apparent to us that the younger and more immature pupils of the public schools may quite properly form a class and be made the subject of this character of legislation. Normal schools and colleges are attended by students who are preparing for serious affairs of life; and being older in years and with wider experience are better fortified to withstand any possible hurtful influence attendant upon membership in secret societies and clubs than the younger pupils attending elementary and secondary schools, who are less experienced and more impressionable.

The district court of appeal, therefore, ruled that the statute of California was adopted to overcome the ill effects of societies on unformed characters and was applicable to all within the designated class, that it did not contravene provisions in the constitutions of California or the United States, and that for those reasons it was valid.

J. P. Waugh for several years affiliated with the Millsaps College chapter of Kappa Sigma Fraternity applied for admission to the law school of the University of Mississippi.[19] With his application for admission he was requested to submit a pledge related to the Mississippi statute prohibiting Greek-letter fraternities and sororities in the educational institutions of the state. Although he stated that he did not intend to encourage ". . . the organization or continuance of any of the prohibited fraternities or of affiliating with or paying dues to any at the University," his refusal to sign a pledge was the grounds upon which he was denied admission to the University of Mississippi.

---

[19] Waugh v. Board of Trustees, Univ. of Miss., 237 US 589, 59 LEd 1131, 35 SCt 720 (1915).

The chancery court of Lafayette County, the Supreme Court of Mississippi, and ultimately the Supreme Court of the United States considered the legality of the pledge which Waugh was asked to sign and which included the statements:

> . . . that he was not pledged to become a member of any of the prohibited fraternities, nor a member of any such; and that he would pledge and promise not to join any such while he was a student, or aid, abet, or encourage the organization or perpetuation of any of the orders. And, further, that he would not apply for nor accept any scholarship or medal or in any way be a beneficiary of any students' self-help fund. That it would be his purpose and constant endeavor so to act that no word or deed of his could be ever remotely construed as being violative of the letter and spirit of the statute.

The Supreme Court of Mississippi reversed the decree of the chancery court which had declared that the statute prohibiting Greek-letter fraternities in the state's educational institutions was "ultra vires, unreasonable, and void" in that it was in violation of the Fourteenth Amendment to the Constitution of the United States. The Supreme Court of the United States, affirming the judgment of the Mississippi Supreme Court, said:

> It is said that the fraternity to which complainant belongs is a moral and of itself a disciplinary force. This need not be denied. But whether such membership makes against discipline was for the state of Mississippi to determine. It is to be remembered that the University was established by the state, and is under the control of the state, and the enactment of the statute may have been induced by the opinion that membership in the prohibited societies divided the attention of the students, and distracted from that singleness of purpose which the state desired to exist in its public educational institutions. It is not for us to entertain conjectures in opposition to the views of the state, and annul its regulations upon disputable considerations of their wisdom or

necessity.   Nor can we accommodate the regulations
to the assertion of a special purpose by the applying
student, varying, perhaps, with each one, and dependent
alone upon his promise.

This being our view of the power of the legislature,
we do not enter upon a consideration of the elements of
complainant's contention.   It is very trite to say that
the right to pursue happiness and exercise rights and
liberty are subject in some degree to the limitations of
the law, and the condition upon which the state of Mississippi offers the complainant free instruction in the
University, that while a student there he renounce affiliation with a society which the state considers inimical to
discipline, finds no prohibition in the 14th Amendment.

In Iowa a school board adopted a resolution essentially
the same as the state statute which prohibited membership
or solicitation of membership in any organization by anyone
enrolled in public schools wholly or partly supported by
state funds unless the organizations were sanctioned by the
proper school authorities.   The resolution provided for
suspension of pupils who belonged to such organizations
after the parents had been notified.   In the case of *Lee
v. Hoffman,* the plaintiffs were seeking restoration as students in the public school after having been excluded as
a result of their membership in prohibited societies.[20]

Justice Salinger, expressing the opinion of the Supreme
Court of Iowa, pointed out the similarity of the rule under
question and the state statute and admonished those who
questioned the validity of rules in direct compliance with
statutory enactments:

   . . . there is nothing unconstitutional about requiring
   an application for permission to join a society.   And if
   the courts, instead of hunting opportunities to declare
   statutes void, seek in every reasonable way to avoid the
   necessity for pronouncing upon their validity, no good
   reason is perceivable why they may not decline to interpret the Constitution for suitors who have hunted,

---

   20 Lee v. Hoffman, 182 Iowa 1216, 166 NW 565 (1918).

instead of attempted to avoid, a controversy over the Constitution—who are before the court only because they refused to do what if done might have made it unnecessary for them to ask the court to construe the Constitution.

The Iowa court found nothing unreasonable nor did it find an excessive use of authority in a board's action which was in direct agreement with a valid statute.

In the case of *Sutton* v. *Board of Education of Springfield,* the· plaintiff sought to discover whether the legislature had the constitutional authority to authorize and direct boards of education to suspend or expel pupils on the basis of membership in a Greek-letter society.[21]   Relying heavily upon the decision made in *University of Mississippi* v. *Waugh,* 105 Miss 623, 62 So 827, the Supreme Court of Illinois declared the anti-fraternity statute valid and stated:

> The statute does not purport to control pupils in their homes or in social activities under the supervision of their parents, but declares that the secret societies and organizations defined therein are inimical to the public good and for that reason they are forbidden. The Legislature considered such societies detrimental to the good order and best interests of the schools, and we cannot say the statute is not a reasonable enactment and a valid exercise of legislative powers for the promotion of the best interests of the schools and the discipline and good order therein.

The mandate to suspend, expel, or withhold credit and a diploma from anyone enrolled in the public school who was a member of a fraternity or sorority was given to local boards of education by the statute adopted by the legislature of Michigan in 1927 which declared membership in secret societies to be unlawful. Although Verne Steele, a senior in the high school and a member of a fraternity was permitted to remain in school, he was denied credit

---

21 Sutton v. Board of Education of Springfield, 306 Ill 507, 138 NE 131 (1923).

which would lead to graduation.[22] Upon questioning it was found that Steele was aware of the penalty to which he had subjected himself, but he challenged the act in the court of law upon the grounds that the title of the act was not inclusive of subject matter in the act, that the act was "cruel and unusual punishment" in denying credit and a diploma which had been earned, that the act deprived him of "liberty" and "property" without due process of law, and that the act denied him the "equal protection of the law."

The Supreme Court of Michigan declared the statute valid indicating that there was no doubt that the fraternity of which Steele was a member was included in the statute which stated that "every such fraternity, sorority, and secret society as herein defined is declared an obstruction to education, inimical to the public welfare, and illegal." The court further pointed out that "loss of right to school credits and a graduate's diploma, based upon a willful violation of the statute, does not, by any stretch of imagination, constitute cruel and unusual punishment." The court was unable to see in the statute a denial of any right granted the plaintiff under the Fourteenth Amendment of the Constitution of the United States.

Of particular interest in this case was the dissenting opinion written by Judge Potter and with which two other members of the court concurred:

> There is no claim the pupil asking relief did not attend the public schools, did not complete the course of study prescribed therein, is not, so far as educational qualifications are concerned, entitled to graduate, in any event, entitled to credit for the work he has done or that his fraternalistic activity interfered in any way with his education or with his study. Under the school system pupils are graded and classified. When a prescribed subject is passed a pupil is entitled to credit therefor. . . .
>
>   *   *   *
>
> . . . Public education has its legitimate sphere, but the child, except when in school or on his way to or from

---

[22] Steele v. Sexton, 253 Mich 32, 234 NW 436 (1931).

there, is not under the control of school authorities. . . . This law arbitrarily interferes with the sphere of individual liberty, guaranteed by the Constitution, seeks to establish unjust, unreasonable, and arbitrary rules of social conduct, and deprives the pupil and his parents of property, in violation of the Constitution of this state and of the Fourteenth Amendment of the Constitution of the United States. . . .

Although several decisions have been rendered in regard to statutes abolishing secret societies, each case differed in some particular from that of another. The resolution of Caddo Parish School Board which was passed five days prior to the opening of school and which required the principal in each school to suspend or expel any pupil who was a member of a secret society was held in accordance with the act of the legislature of Louisiana which permitted local boards to abolish sororities and fraternities in the public schools.[23] Since the children involved were above the compulsory school age, the similarity of circumstances in *Hughes* v. *Caddo Parish School Board* and in *Waugh* v. *Board of Trustees, Univ. of Miss.*[24] prompted the United States Supreme Court to affirm the judgment of the lower court validating the Louisiana statute in a per curiam decision.

The Supreme Court of Florida was requested to issue a declaratory decree as to the status of the Satan Fraternity under the statutory provision barring secret organizations in the public schools.[25] The court found no merit in the plaintiffs' statements that the title of the act was insufficient to denote the contents and that it deprived the appellants of their right to life, liberty, pursuit of happiness, due process of law, free speech, free assembly, and redress of grievances.

---

[23] Hughes v. Caddo Parish School Board, 57 FSupp 508 (WD La., 1944), aff'd 323 US 685, 65 SCt 562 (1945).

[24] Waugh v. Board of Trustees, Univ. of Miss., supra n 19.

[25] Satan Fraternity v. Board of Public Instruction for Dade County, 156 Fla 222, 22 S(2d) 892 (1945).

Stating that similar acts in other states had been upheld in courts of law, that the conduct and discipline of public schools were vested in board of public instruction, and that it was beyond the purpose of the courts to consider the reasonableness of legislative enactments, the court saw no reason to interfere with the action that had been taken. In affirmation of the lower court's judgment, Justice Terrell, expressing the majority opinion of the Supreme Court of Florida, said:

> We cannot see that the question of state vs. parental control enters into the picture in any manner. The public school system has a very definite place in our scheme of things and the question in every case is whether or not the high school fraternity or sorority disrupts or materially interferes with that purpose. . . . there has long been a feeling in this country that this question requires an affirmative answer, and the legislature has concluded the matter in this state.

In discussing submission of rights of individuals, Justice Terrell commented:

> . . . it is pertinent to state that none of our liberties are absolutes; all of them may be limited when the common good or common decency requires. . . . Freedom after all is not something turned footloose to run as it will like a thoroughbred in a blue grass meadow. Freedom in a democracy is a matter of character and tolerance. The ideal recipient of it is one who voluntarily refuses to sacrifice the common good to personal possession.

One of the most lengthy trials in the history of litigation pertaining to secret societies was *Burkitt* v. *School District No. 1, Multnowah County,* which lasted about two weeks and in which there was almost one thousand pages of testimony.[26] Although a statute was enacted in 1909 declaring that secret organizations "of every kind and character" were

---

[26] Burkitt v. School Dist. No. 1, Multnomah County, 195 Ore 471, 246 P(2d) 566 (1952).

unlawful, it was not until 1936 that the city of Portland, Oregon, made a serious attempt to uphold the statute by requesting pupils and their parents to sign a pledge indicating that the pupil was not and would not become a member of a secret society while enrolled in the public schools of Portland.

Protests against the pledge system led to its abandonment, and school officials did not again attempt to restrict membership in secret societies until they began to detect the influence of the societies in school affairs. In 1949 another resolution, stating as a penalty for membership in a secret society suspension or expulsion, was adopted by the board of education. This resolution with eighteen rules governing the creation and maintenance of organizations was the point for litigation in the plaintiffs' declaration that the board had misinterpreted the statute. The plaintiffs claimed that the organizations in question were not secret and that the rule was arbitrary, discriminatory, violated the right of assemblage, and was an invasion of parental authority since the clubs met outside of school hours.

The Supreme Court of Oregon found the rule within the authority of the school board, reasonable, and enacted in good faith. In rendering the decision in favor of the school board, the Supreme Court called attention to the fact that by enrolling in and attending the public schools, the pupils came under the control and discipline of school officials who were in a position to determine what was "inimical to the discipline and effective operation of the schools." Elaborating on its statement, the court ruled:

> When they avail themselves of that opportunity they must, in the nature of things, submit to the discipline of the schools and to regulations reasonably calculated to promote such discipline and the high purpose for which the schools are established—the education of youth, which is not limited to the imparting of knowledge, but includes as well the development of character and preparation for the assumption of the responsibilities of citizenship in a democracy. To attain these ends not the least in value of the lessons to be learned are the

lessons of self-restraint, self-discipline, tolerance, and respect for duly constituted authority. In this regard parents and the schools have their respective rights and duties, which complement one another, and may be exercised and discharged in cooperation for the welfare of the child and the state.

Here, as it seems to us, for the court to interfere with the action of the school authorities now challenged would be little less than to constitute ourselves a school board for all the schools of the state. This is something we have neither the right nor the inclination to do.

The court of appeals of Ohio in April, 1962, was called upon to review the circumstances of a case in which parents brought a class suit on behalf of their minor children to petition the court for a permanent injunction to enjoin the school board of Columbus, Ohio, from enforcing a regulation which prohibited any pupil attending the public school and holding membership in a fraternity or sorority from participating in ". . . any athletic, literary, military, musical, dramatic, service, scientific, scholastic, and other similar activities of his school, including honor societies or honor organizations."[27] In addition such pupils were declared ineligible to hold office in their class or school; to receive any honor, scholastic or otherwise; or to represent the school in any manner.

The plaintiffs objected to the regulation on the grounds that if the regulation were enforced the school authorities would gain complete control of the pupils' activities and thus deny parents their responsibility to select associates for their children away from school and after school hours. Also mentioned in the case was that the enforcement of the regulation would deny pupils their rights to participate in the activities of a public school. The school board answered the objections by stating that the organizations mentioned had a divisive influence in the school and presented problems to the school authorities.

---

[27] Holroyd v. Eibling, 116 OhioApp 440, 188 NE(2d) 797 (1962); appeal dism 186 NE(2d) 200 (1962).

Citing the Ohio statute which placed a fine on any pupil who organized, joined, or held membership in a fraternity or sorority and referring to previous cases involving pupil membership in secret organizations, the court upheld the authority of the school board to adopt the regulation and found no merit in the contentions of those who brought the case.

§ 2.3 Antifraternity rules and regulations in the absence of specific statutes

An examination of judicial decisions which explore the reasonableness and constitutionality of regulatory and prohibitory rules concerning membership in secret societies indicates that school authorities, feeling secure in the existence of supporting legislation and attempting to execute legislative directives to abolish or to limit membership in secret societies in the public schools, enacted rules and regulations which when challenged in court were declared valid and within the power of the boards. In some states, however, school officials have been unable to rely upon specific legislative enactments forbidding secret societies in the state supported schools. In these instances where boards of education have been requested to prohibit such organizations because of their detrimental effect on the government and control of the schools in their jurisdiction, boards have sought solutions to the problem through administrative acts not sanctioned by specific statutory provision. In the absence of special statutory authority, the officials of the school have claimed the authority for and justification of their actions under the broad discretionary powers delegated by the state to those responsible for the government and control of school districts.

Rules banning secret societies seldom meet with universal approval from pupils, parents, and other citizens. Out of the dissatisfactions with board actions have grown opportunities for the courts to render judicial interpretations which have established certain legal principles concerning the authority and power of school officials to restrict membership in secret societies without specific statutory authorization.

The earliest recorded case dealing with secret societies involved Wheaton College, a private institution, whose charter gave the trustees and faculty the power and authority ". . . to adopt and enforce such rules as may be deemed expedient for the government of the institution."[28] A writ of mandamus to compel Wheaton College to reinstate E. Hartley Pratt, who violated a college rule by holding membership in a secret society, was denied by the courts. Refusing to issue the writ, Mr. Justice Lawrence in his dicta said:

> We perceive nothing unreasonable in the rule itself, since all persons familiar with college life know that the tendency of secret societies is to withdraw students from the control of the faculty, and impair to some extent the discipline of the institution. . . . A discretionary power has been given them to regulate the discipline of their college in such manner as they deem proper, and so long as their rules violate neither divine nor human law, we have no more authority to interfere than we have to control the domestic discipline of a father in his family. . . . When it is said that a person has a legal *right* to do certain things, all that phrase means is, that the law does not forbid these things to be done. It does not mean that the law guarantees the right to do them at all possible times and under all possible circumstances. . . . The son of the relator has undoubtedly legal rights to join either Wheaton College or the Good Templars, and they have both an undoubted right to expel him if he refuses to abide by such regulations as they establish, not inconsistent with law or good morals.

In the latter part of the nineteenth century the Supreme Court of Indiana reversed the judgment of the Tippecanoe circuit court when it declared a rule that denied a student admission to Purdue University, a tax-supported institution, by reason of his refusal to sign a pledge stating his intention to withdraw from a fraternity of which he was

---

[28] Illinois ex rel Pratt v. Wheaton College, 40 Ill 186 (1866).

a member "ultra vires" and "palpably unreasonable."[29] Distinguishing between the control of a pupil's activity after admission and before admission to the institution, the judge said:

> If mere membership in any so-called Greek fraternities may be treated as a disqualification for admission as a student in a public school, then membership in any secret or similar society may be converted into a like disqualification, and in this way discrimination might be made against large classes of the inhabitants of the State, in utter disregard of the fundamental ideas upon which our entire educational system is based.

A dissenting judge indicated that he was unable to detect the difference in granting the power to expel a student

If the moment a student has passed the portal of the who did not obey the rules of the institution and in permitting the exclusion of a student who refused to obey the rules if admitted by saying:

> institution he is bound to obey a prescribed rule of the college, he may, in all reason, be required, before he is permitted to enter, to promise obedience. The final remedy for disobedience is expulsion, and, if there may be expulsion for disobeying, there may be exclusion for refusing to promise compliance with a proper regulation.

The Supreme Court of Washington upheld the local school district rule to prohibit fraternity members from taking part in extracurricular activities in *Wayland* v. *Board of School Directors of Dist. No. 1 of Seattle.*[30] The testimony of the principal, the president of the school board, and other school authorities gave support to the defendants' brief that fraternities and sororities had had an adverse effect on the government and good conduct of Seattle High School. An editorial from a quarterly publication of the fraternity in question served to substantiate the respondents' claim that

---

[29] Indiana ex rel Stallard v. White, 82 Ind 278 (1882).

[30] Wayland v. Board of School Directors of Dist. No. 1 of Seattle, 43 Wash 441, 86 Pac 642 (1906).

fraternity membership often resulted in insubordination to proper school authorities.

In denying privileges other than classroom instruction to students who refused to pledge that they were not members of a secret society, the school board was acting in good faith; its actions were ". . . at all times general in application and at no time special, malicious or arbitrary . . ." as was contended by the plaintiffs. The respondents were acting within their authority, ruled the court:

> The board has not invaded the homes of any pupils, nor have they sought to interfere with parental custody and control. They have not said these fraternities shall not meet at the various homes, nor have they attempted to control students out of school hours. The evidence shows beyond a doubt that these secret organizations when effected foster a clannish spirit of insubordination, which results in much evil to the good order, harmony, discipline, and general welfare of the school.

A resolution adopted by the board of education in Chicago which denied public recognition of fraternities and sororities, including the privilege of meeting in the school, and which deprived fraternity and sorority members of representing the school in any public capacity was attacked as being arbitrary, unreasonable, discriminatory, and in violation of natural rights by Eberle Wilson in his appeal to enjoin the board of education from enforcing the rule.[31] Since there was no specific statutory provision for such a rule, the board assumed its authority from its responsibility to maintain an "efficient" system of schools and its duty ". . . to establish all such by-laws, rules, and regulations for the government and for the establishment and maintenance of a proper and uniform system of discipline in the several schools as may, in their opinion, be necessary."

The Supreme Court of the state held that the rule was neither unlawful nor unreasonable. It was pointed out that pupils who attend the public schools of Chicago must

---

31 Wilson v. Board of Education of Chicago, 233 Ill 464, 84 NE 697 (1908).

make a decision whether they prefer fraternity membership or the privilege to represent their school in literary and athletic contests or in any other public capacity.

Shortly after the judgment was made in favor of the Board of Education of Chicago, a similar case arose concerning the same rule and presented the same points for consideration. The Supreme Court of Illinois, citing the similarity of the two cases, affirmed the judgment of the lower court in a per curiam decision in *Favorite* v. *Board of Education of Chicago*.[32]

One of the few decisions which does not uphold the school board's authority to exclude pupils who are members of secret societies from extracurricular activities is found in *Wright* v. *Board of Education*.[33]   In 1920 the St. Louis Board of Education adopted a resolution stating its opposition to the existence, formation, and joining of secret societies in the schools of that city. The action by the board was provoked by the superintendent's statement:

> Secret organizations in the high schools are undemocratic and undesirable and injurious to the free and wholesome life of these schools. They exert a pernicious influence upon their own members and upon pupils who do not belong to them, and upon the voluntary organizations of pupils, that are approved and fostered by the schools, and they are subversive of the fundamental principles upon which the public schools rest.

During the year a penalty for membership was subscribed by the superintendent in his recommendation which was adopted by the school board ". . . that high-school pupils who refuse to conform to this regulation be declared ineligible to membership in organizations authorized and fostered by the school; that they be not permitted to represent the school in any capacity whatsoever; and that they be not allowed to participate in graduation exercises."

----

32 Favorite v. Board of Education of Chicago, 235 Ill 314, 85 NE 402 (1908).

33 Wright v. Board of Education of St. Louis, 295 Mo 466, 246 SW 43 (1922).

Although testimony was presented by the school officials alleging that fraternity members made lower grades than non-fraternity members, the Missouri court discounted some of the testimony and ruled that there was insufficient evidence to prove that secret societies were a detriment to the efficient operation of the schools. The Supreme Court further stated that under the general authority which was granted to local boards of control one could not assume power not "clearly inferable from the purpose of the act" and that the school's domain ". . . ceases when the child reaches its home unless its act is such as to affect the conduct and discipline of the school." The court indicated that "any other interpretation would remove all limit to the exercise of discretionary power, leave it to the judgment, whim, or caprice of each succeeding board."

A Massachusetts statute provided that the school committee ". . . may supervise and control all athletics and other organizations composed of public school pupils and bearing the school name or organized in connection therewith."[34] With attention focused upon this statute, the high court in Massachusetts upheld the school committee of Haverhill in its expulsion of several students who violated their pledge regarding membership in secret societies.

The petitioners challenged the right of the committee to pass and enforce a rule which forbade membership in secret societies not approved by the local superintendent and principal, which banned the wearing of insignia and apparel of unapproved societies on the school premises, and which required organizations of the school to submit certain information regarding club activities. The court, in dismissing the petition, ruled that the expulsion of the students did not exceed the power conferred to the committee and further reasoned:

The power to make rules would be vain without the capacity to annex reasonable penalties for their violation. Rules adopted by the constituted authorities for

---

[34] Antell v. Stokes, 287 Mass 103, 191 NE 407 (1934).

the governance of public schools must be presumed to be based upon mature deliberation and for the welfare of the community. A pupil who persistently violates such rules, especially after having made express promise to obey them, may be excluded from the school by the school committee acting in good faith. No personal right stands superior to the public welfare in this particular.

Not unlike many school districts, the school district in Durham, North Carolina, adopted a pledge system in its battle against secret societies. Whether refusal to sign a pledge declaring non-membership in a fraternity constituted grounds for exclusion of a pupil from participation in the extracurricular activities of the school was the question raised in *Coggin* v. *Board of Education of Durham*.[35] The parents residing in the school district were notified that since the board's public expression of disapproval of sororities and fraternities had not been effective in their elimination, that it was necessary to adopt more effective measures ". . . to eradicate from our schools influences that are harmful to the existence and promotion of real democratic ideals and proper social behavior." With this preface the school officials presented the pledge which pupils would be required to sign in order to be permitted to enjoy the full privileges of the school. Pupils who were not willing to state that they were not members and would not become members of any societies not approved by the board and that they would not attend nor give financial support to any meetings or social affairs of such societies were denied participation in extracurricular activities which included:

Holding any office of Student Body, Homeroom Class or Club.

Taking part in all intramural and interscholastic activities or contests, both athletic and literary.

Representing the school or class or any organization in any capacity.

---

[35] Coggin v. Board of Education of City of Durham, 223 NC 765, 28 SE(2d) 527 (1944).

Serving as Editors and Managers of any school publications, or writing articles therefor.

Taking part in the Senior play or other dramatic activities.

Participating in Assembly or Homeroom programs.

Serving as Cafeteria or Library helper.

Attending High School dances or socials.

Serving as Monitors in any capacity.

Becoming a member of any school-sponsored club, society, or organization.

J. R. Coggin, a member of Phi Kappa Delta, did not sign the pledge and was denied the privilege of playing football and participating in the other activities mentioned previously. Justice Barnhill, rendering the decision for the Supreme Court of North Carolina, emphasized that attendance at a public school was not an absolute right and that:

> Schools to be effective and fulfill the purposes for which they are intended must be operated in an orderly manner. Machinery to that end must be provided. Reasonable rules and regulations must be adopted. The right to attend school and claim the benefits afforded by the public school system is the right to attend subject to all lawful rules and regulations prescribed for the government thereof.

                    *   *   *

> The rule makes no attempt to deny plaintiff any instruction afforded by class work or by the required curriculum of the school. Nor is he denied the right to participate in extra-curricular activities. It is merely made optional with him to determine whether, against the known wishes of the school authorities, he prefers to continue his membership in a secret society and thereby forfeit participation in the privileges afforded by the extra-curricular activities of the school, which, by compliance with the rule, would be available to him. He has now arrived at one of the crossroads of life. He must decide which course he will take, and the choice is his.

. . . it will be kept in mind that the local board is the final authority so long as it acts in good faith and refrains from adopting regulations which are clearly arbitrary or unreasonable. . . .

If the opinion of the court or jury is to be substituted for the judgment and discretion of the board at the will of a disaffected pupil, the government of our schools will be seriously impaired, and the position of school boards in dealing with such cases will be most precarious.. The Court, therefore, will not consider whether such rules and regulations are wise or expedient. Nor will it interfere with the exercise of the sound discretion of school trustees in matters confided by law to their discretion.

A pledge similar to that exacted from pupils in Durham was challenged as being discriminatory against fraternity and sorority members, arbitrary, oppressive, unreasonable, and illegal.[36] The pledge, required of junior and senior high school pupils, once signed was to remain effective until graduation of the pupil and to apply to periods of vacation. The class suit brought to enjoin the enforcement of the rule passed by the board of trustees was refused an injunction by the lower court; and upon appeal to the court of civil appeals of Texas, the plaintiffs were told that the rule was within the legal exercise of power delegated to local trustees by the legislature with one exception—the extension of the rule into vacation periods.

The court ruled that such an extension of discretionary authority would be "practically unenforceable" and ". . . to extend the rule of loco parentis to such length . . . would be shocking to every concept of parental authority."

The court in *Isgrig* v. *Srygley* upheld the antifraternity rule which made pupils in Little Rock High School holding membership in secret societies, ineligible for class offices, club membership, and scholastic or class honors.[37] Flagrant

---

[36] Wilson v. Abilene Independent School Dist., 190 SW(2d) 406 (Tex, 1945).

[37] Isgrig v. Srygley, 210 Ark 580, 197 SE(2d) 39 (1946).

abuse of the rule and open defiance of school authority prompted the court to say:

A situation of this kind was not contemplated by those who provided a free school system. Some one, at some point, must hold a responsible hand; and some one must say to our maturing citizens that barter by threat is not an approved method of procuring results. This is particularly true when the thing sought to be approved has been put to the student body and emphatically voted down, as fraternities and sororities were just before the resolution of 1945 was adopted.

Conceding, as any one who reasons must, that group organizations may promote efficiency, and in some instances inculcate a sense of responsibility in young men and young women who have reached in life's span a period of juvenile dependability, it does not follow that School Directors are without authority to impose reasonable restrictions in those instances where experience, observation, and a knowledge of the personality being dealt with suggest this course.

Under a resolution adopted by the Board of Trustees of the State University of New York, the president of the institution was authorized to take any steps which he deemed appropriate in banning social organizations which were affiliated in any way with organizations outside of the school and which denied membership to students because of race, color, creed, religion, nationality, or other "artificial" criteria.[38] A member of a national fraternity was unsuccessful in his attempt to seek a judgment declaring the rule unconstitutional because it was a violation of civil rights, freedom of assembly, and equal protection of the law, was adopted without due process of law, and adversely affected existing contracts. To the contrary, the court was unable to find grounds for declaring the rule unconstitutional; and in the language of the court it was ruled that "a state may adopt such measures, including the outlawing of certain social organizations, as it deems necessary to

---

[38] Webb v. State Univ. of New York, 125 FSupp 910 (ND NY, 1954).

its duty of supervision and control of its educational institutions."

§ 2.4 Summary

The court more than ninety years ago was called upon to express its opinion concerning the legality of an anti-fraternity rule. Since that time, individuals and groups have petitioned the courts on numerous occasions to settle the conflicts arising out of state legislation or local school rules dealing with membership in secret societies. Litigation has not been confined to any particular area of the United States nor has it been limited to the jurisdiction of state courts only. Legislation and local rules have been tested in the appellate courts of seventeen states in the past century and in two instances have reached the Supreme Court of the United States. In each case the court, reluctant to interfere with the operation of the schools, has not attempted to pass upon the wisdom or expediency of the rules in question; but rather the court has rendered its judgment solely upon its consideration of the reasonableness and constitutionality of the actions taken.

Declaring that secret societies were detrimental to the operation, discipline, and good order of the public educational institutions, those charged with managing the schools have adopted rules and regulations which may be categorized according to the penalties imposed for violation. Categorization of the cases might, therefore, include cases that deal with: denying admittance to pupils to public educational institutions solely on the basis of their membership in secret societies (the cases reported deal with colleges only); suspension or expulsion of pupils because of their membership in secret societies; withholding credit earned from pupils because of their membership in secret societies; and denying participation of sorority or fraternity members in activities other than actual classroom instruction.

In 1882, the Supreme Court of Indiana said to Purdue University in *Indiana ex rel. Stallard* v. *White, supra*, n 29 that the rule of the board of trustees was "ultra vires" and "palpably unreasonable" in disqualifying a pupil for admission to the tax-supported school solely on the basis of his membership in a Greek-letter fraternity and his refusal to sign a pledge to withdraw from the fraternity during his enrollment at Purdue University. The decision of the Indiana court became of little consequence when twenty-three years later the Supreme Court of the United States in *Waugh* v. *Board of Trustees, Univ. of Miss., supra,* n 19, affirmed the judgment of the Mississippi Supreme Court which upheld the University of Mississippi in denying admittance to a pupil who refused to sign a pledge related to the antifraternity statute of Mississippi. The United States Supreme Court stated that the action taken was not in contravention of the Fourteenth Amendment and that it was the responsibility, and within the authority, of the state to decide whether fraternities had such an effect upon its educational institutions as to warrant such a statute.

Although a specific antifraternity statute did not exist, the court in *Illinois ex rel. Pratt* v. *Wheaton College,* 1866, *supra,* n 28, refused to grant a writ of mandamus to reinstate a boy who had been suspended for holding membership in a secret society against the expressed rules of the college. After this first decision was made concerning the suspension and expulsion of pupils who disobeyed antifraternity rules, every decade in the twentieth century with the exception of one was to find the courts in various states considering the authority of boards of education to suspend or expel pupils on the basis of their membership in secret societies:

1912 - *Bradford* v. *Board of Education of City and County of San Francisco, supra,* n 17. The district court of appeals of California ruled that the statute which had been adopted in California to overcome the ill effects of secret societies was not contrary to the constitutions of California or United States, was not illegal class legislation, and was, therefore, valid.

1918 - *Lee* v. *Hoffman, supra,* n 20. The Supreme Court of Iowa found that the school board rule in question was reasonable and was in compliance with the state statute; in that it was in agreement with the statute the rule was not considered an excessive exertion of power by the school board.

1923 - *Sutton* v. *Board of Education of Springfield, supra,* n 21. Relying heavily upon the *Waugh* case, the Supreme Court of Illinois declared the antifraternity statute which provided for suspension or expulsion of pupils holding membership in secret societies valid and upheld the authority of the legislature to authorize and direct boards of education to suspend or expel fraternity and sorority members if it was in the best interest of the schools.

1934 - *Antell* v. *Stokes, supra,* n 34. Although Massachusetts did not have a statute specifically prohibiting secret societies in the public school, it did have a statute providing the school committee with the authority to supervise and manage the organizations and athletics of the school. The Massachusetts court, upholding the school committee in the expulsion of a pupil who violated the pledge taken concerning secret societies, ruled that with the power to make rules goes the power to enforce them.

1945 - *Hughes* v. *Caddo Parish School Board, supra,* n 23. The United States Supreme Court sustained the judgment of the Supreme Court of Louisiana in a per curiam decision which upheld the school board's authority to suspend or expel pupils in secret societies in accordance with the statute giving power to local boards to abolish secret societies.

1945 - *Satan Fraternity* v. *Board of Public Instruction for Dade County, supra,* n 25. The Supreme Court of Florida, giving judicial cognizance to judgments in similar cases, declared the antifraternity rule in question was not a deprivation of the right to life, liberty, pursuit of happiness, freedom of speech, freedom of assembly, redress of grievances, or due process of law as charged.

1952 - *Burkitt* v. *School District No. 1, Multnomah County, supra,* n 26. The Supreme Court of Oregon in upholding the authority of the board of education to suspend a pupil said that the antifraternity rule enacted by the local school authorities of Portland was supported by the statute, was reasonable, and was enacted in good faith.

1954 - *Webb* v. *State University of New York, supra,* n 38. The United States district court upheld the Board of Trustees of the State University of New York in delegating to its president the authority to take any action which he deemed appropriate in banning social organizations which were affiliated with organizations outside of the school and which denied membership to students because of some "artificial" criteria.

The Supreme Court of Michigan in *Steele* v. *Sexton, supra,* n 22 discounted the claim by the plaintiff that withholding credits and diploma because of membership in a secret society constituted "cruel and unusual punishment" and was a deprivation of "liberty," "property," and "equal protection of the law." The court ruled that the denial of credit and a diploma by the board was based upon the student's willful violation of a valid statute which directed the board to take such action.

In the absence of antifraternity statutes school authorities, in an attempt to restrict the membership of pupils in secret societies, have relied heavily upon confining the activities of fraternity and sorority members to classroom instruction. The first challenge of this regulatory action to reach the higher courts came in Washington with *Wayland* v. *Board of School Directors of District No. 1 of Seattle, supra,* n 30. The testimony of the high school principal, the president of the school board, and other school authorities sufficed to convince the Supreme Court of Washington that secret societies had tended to foster a spirit of insubordination toward school authorities and were, therefore, detrimental to the discipline and good order of the school.

The Supreme Court of Illinois in *Wilson* v. *Board of Education of Chicago, supra,* n 31, found nothing unlawful or unreasonable in the board's rule which forbade fraternity and sorority members' participation in extracurricular activities, which refused public recognition to fraternities and sororities, and which forbade members of such societies to represent the school in any public capacity. In the same year the same court found the identical questions in *Favorite* v. *Board of Education of Chicago, supra,* n 32, and upheld the school board's action in a per curiam decision.

The one occasion in which the courts ruled against the action taken by a board of education to exclude members of sororities and fraternities from participation in extracurricular activities, graduation exercises, and public activities of the school is found in *Wright* v. *Board of Education of St. Louis, supra,* n 33. The Supreme Court of Missouri found insufficient evidence that the societies had a disrupting effect on the operation of the school; and since authority to enact the regulation was not "clearly inferable" in the statutes, the judgment was in favor of the plaintiffs.

A North Carolina court in *Coggin* v. *Board of Education of Durham, supra,* n 35 found refusal to sign a pledge concerning secret societies grounds for banning participation in extracurricular activities of the school. In rendering its decision, the Supreme Court of North Carolina reminded the plaintiffs that the school board was the final authority in that the rule was not unreasonable or arbitrary and that the board had acted in good faith.

A similar pledge was the target for litigation in *Wilson* v. *Abilene Independent School District, supra,* n 36. The court of civil appeals of Texas ruled in favor of the board of education with one exception. The court saw in the restriction of pupils during vacation periods an undue invasion of parental authority.

The Supreme Court of Arkansas in *Isgrig* v. *Srygley, supra,* n 37, following the precedent set by other courts, upheld the antifraternity rule which made pupils holding membership in secret societies ineligible for class office, club membership, school and class honors. A similar decision was rendered by the court of appeals of Ohio when another such regulation adopted by the school board was challenged in *Holroyd* v. *Eibling, supra,* n 27.

Since rendering the first judgment in 1866, the courts have been petitioned on numerous occasions to determine the reasonableness and constitutionality of various antifraternity rules and regulations. From the literature related to the control of secret societies in the public schools, one may surmise that the courts have not reviewed the issues involved for the last time; however, one studying previous court decisions concerning the subject may predict with a fair amount of accuracy the outcome of future litigation.

Chapter 3

LEGALITY OF RULES AND REGULATIONS CONCERNING THE ATTENDANCE AND PARTICIPATION OF MARRIED PUPILS IN VARIOUS SCHOOL ACTIVITIES

Section
3.1 Teenage marriage, a challenge to educators
3.2 Authority of school boards to compel married pupils to attend school
3.3 Authority of school boards to exclude married pupils from school attendance
3.4 Authority of school boards to exclude married pupils from participation in extracurricular activities
3.5 Summary

In this day of competition for leadership among the nations of the world in the economic, social, political, and scientific areas of living, it is rather surprising to find that there are many who do not take equal pride in knowing that the United States leads the modern industrial societies in having the youngest average age for marriage.[1] The median age of first marriage for males in the United States in 1890 was 26.1 and for females, 22.0;[2] by 1961 the median age of first marriage had changed to 22.8 for males and 20.3 for females.[3] With the increase in the number of early marriages, with the increase in the enrollment in the public schools, and with the social and economic pressures being placed on the desire for a high school diploma have come problems heretofore unknown to the schools. It is not unusual that educators are expressing a particular concern in relation to the role of the school in helping these young people who marry early to adjust to their new lives and at the same time in finding some way to discourage other marriages among pupils with whom they come in

---

[1] Robert Havighurst, "Early Marriages and the Schools," The School Review, LXIX (Spring, 1961), p. 36.

[2] U. S. Bureau of Census, Historical Statistics of the United States, Colonial Times to 1957 (Washington, D. C.: United States Government Printing Office, 1960), p. 15.

[3] U. S. Bureau of Census, Statistical Abstract of the United States: 1962 (Washington, D. C.: United States Government Printing Office, 1962), p. 72.

contact; nor is it unusual to find varying opinions as to the best course of action to take concerning the future attendance and participation of these young people in the public school program.

Witnessing a teenage marriage, Buscher notes:

Society had evidenced its approval of the marriage by issuing a license to wed. The state, recognizing the right of the parents to act for offspring under legal age, had insisted only on negative blood tests and a three-day waiting period. The minister, by the ceremony, was bestowing the approval of the church.[4]

Inquiries concerning the trend in the direction of earlier marriages have been made by those seeking an explanation for the change. Landis found an answer to such an inquiry in the response he received from 286 principals. Factors which the principals felt had influenced student marriage rates included:[5]

1. Increase in parental laxity and poor home conditions;
2. Compulsory military service for young men and indefinite plans for the future;
3. Increased acceptance of the idea that marriage will solve all problems;
4. Insecurity of these times;
5. Effect of a student marriage on others;
6. Prosperity and employment opportunities for young people;
7. Availability of young employed men;
8. Acceptance of early marriage by parents and community;
9. Desire to attain the status and privileges of adults;
10. Emphasis placed on sex by mass media;
11. Fear of not marrying;
12. Early maturity of youth socially and psychologically;

---

4 Velora Buscher, "Forsaking All Others," NEA Journal, XLIV (February, 1955), p. 76.

5 Judson Landis, "Attitudes and Policies Concerning Marriages Among High School Students," Marriage and Family Living, XVIII (May, 1956), p. 130.

13. Going steady;
14. Schools' permissive attitudes toward marriage;
15. Failure in school;
16. Premarital pregnancy;
17. Compulsory school attendance;
18. Ease of obtaining a divorce;
19. Accepted pattern in last year of high school;
20. Society's acceptance of working women.

Certainly, in the preceding enumeration of the factors contributing to the increase in teenage marriages, there is variety. The many theories which are urged by those presenting reasons for early marriages may be incorporated into two basic thoughts:[6]

1. The increased emphasis given to marriage and family life in recent years—This belief has led many to feel that marriage is the "be-all and end-all of human existence." An exaggeration of this belief may be found in those who delegate homemaking as the only career for women and subjugate all the activities of men to their roles of husband and father. Widespread acceptance of this belief would result in an increase in all marriages.

2. The acceleration in all areas of social life in recent years—Children are being "pushed into social maturity" by being encouraged to attend parties, to use cosmetics, to have dates, and to take part in other activities which were at one time confined to participation by adults.

§ 3.1 Teenage marriage, a challenge to educators

Whatever the underlying reasons may be for the increase in youthful marriages, educators throughout the country are facing new challenges created by the growing number of married young people who wish to continue their schooling. With the increase in the number of teenage marriages in the past several years, concern for the welfare not only of these young people marrying but for their associates as well has grown. Many persons contend that

------

6 Richard Kerckhoff and Evelyn Rimel, "Early Marriage, What's All the Fuss About?" The Clearing House, XXVI (May, 1962), p. 460.

if pupils who marry are permitted to take part in the regular school program, other young people will follow their example of early marriage. Others feel that these young people of school age should not be denied the opportunities offered by the public schools. A reflection of the different attitudes of educators may be seen in the provisions made concerning married pupils. Courses in marriage preparation have made their appearance in some schools while others have adopted restrictive policies of a preventive or punitive nature in dealing with married pupils.

Many administrators who advocate the adoption of restrictive measures, which include forced withdrawal from school, enrollment in special classes or schools, or limited participation in school activities, justify their positions by pointing out the problems which they feel are peculiar to married pupils. They indicate that married pupils exert an undesirable influence on other pupils, discuss affairs of a personal nature, attend school irregularly, do not participate in extracurricular activities, expect special concessions, become pregnant or create rumors of pregnancy, are poor in scholarship, and bring criticism of the school from the community. In the 1959-60 school year 117 principals in North Carolina made a comparison of the married pupils in their schools before and after marriage; a compilation of their comparisons showed:[7]

1. All but one principal stated that conduct either improved or remained the same after marriage.

2. All but seven principals said that attitudes toward school improved or stayed the same after marriage.

3. About one-third of the principals said the attendance was worse after marriage.

4. All but eight principals indicated that scholarship improved or remained the same after marriage.

5. About one-fifth of the principals saw acceptance by classmates less after marriage.

---

[7] Gilbert Carroll, "The Status of Married Students in the North Carolina Public High Schools" (unpublished Ed. D. dissertation, Department of Education, Duke University, 1960), p. 31.

6. About one-half of the principals indicated that participation in extracurricular activities was less after marriage.

Of the 286 principals questioned by Landis, some expressed the opinion that the presence of married pupils had some beneficial effects upon the school operation. Those who felt that married pupils were an asset to the school gave as some of their reasons:[8] (1) married pupils are more stable, dependable, mature, industrious, and serious in purpose; (2) married pupils can make a contribution to certain classes, i.e., group guidance classes, family living classes, homemaking classes; (3) married pupils' maturity has a good effect on other pupils; (4) married pupils help others see the reliabilities of marriage; (5) other pupils who marry feel encouraged to continue in school; and (6) married pupils participate in school activities.

When questioned about the policy of the school in dealing with students who marry, the same group of principals gave responses which covered a wide range and which included: have no established policy; no action taken; hold conferences with the married students; place married students on probation; encourage continuance in school; encourage withdrawal; request withdrawal; expel; suspend; advise transfer to a special school; exclude from school office and honors; restrict social activities at school; and permit part-time attendance.[9] Many school boards have adopted specific policies to deal with student marriages while some administrators have taken action without official sanction. Carroll found in a survey of superintendents in North Carolina that almost one-half of them claimed that their administrative unit had a definite policy relating to married students but that less than one-fourth had written school board policies.[10]

Although it is not the purpose of this study to consider the wisdom of various actions relating to student marriage, one cannot refrain, as he reviews the positions taken to

---

8 Landis, "Attitudes and Policies Concerning Marriages Among High School Students," supra n 5, p. 134.

9 Ibid, p. 131.

10 Carroll, "The Status of Married Students in the North Carolina Public High Schools," supra, n 7, p. 104.

discourage students from marrying, from questioning the effectiveness of permissive or restrictive policies. To the knowledge of the writers very little research has been completed in this area; however, Burchinal conducted a survey of the Iowa schools to see if restrictive attendance policies had affected marriage rates in the schools.[11] He found ". . . that restrictive policies are not successful in preventing or even curtailing high school marriages."[12]

As the number of early marriages has increased, school authorities having new problems posed have sought counsel and advice from many sources. Few, if any, states have statutes to guide officials in the decisions that they must make; but since World War II many have requested and received opinions from the attorneys general in various states concerning the status of the married student.[13] Realizing there are limitations imposed by the paucity of cases involving pupil marriage, one may still find some guidance of a legal nature in taking cognizance of the opinions rendered by the courts.

§ 3.2 Authority of school boards to compel married pupils to attend school

Although a great deal of concern has been expressed over the ever-increasing number of early marriages of students, there have been in reality only a few instances of litigation reported. In this century only eleven cases dealing directly with teenage marriages and the schools have appeared in the higher courts, seven being since 1957. Because most young people who marry are past the age of compulsory school attendance, most cases have been concerned with the exclusion of pupils from school or various school activities rather than from forcing children to attend school; however, the courts have had to consider the question of whether under the compulsory school law, present in most states, the child who marries before he attains the

---

[11] Lee G. Burchinal, "Do Restrictive Policies Curb Teen Marriages?" Overview, I (March, 1960), pp. 72 to 73.

[12] Ibid., p. 73.

[13] Howard Matthews, "The Courts and Married Students," School Life, XLIV (November-December, 1961), p. 5.

age when he may legally withdraw from school may be
required to attend school.

In 1946 the Supreme Court of Louisiana in *State* v. *Priest*
first dealt with the problem of compulsory attendance of
married students.[14]   Louise Davis Priest, who was fifteen
on March 26, 1946, had been committed to the State Industrial School for Girls at Alexandria, Louisiana, charged
with juvenile delinquency consisting of "continued truancy"
from the school in which she was enrolled.   Although the
young lady was married November 14, 1945, the judge of
the juvenile court ruled that marriage did not exempt her
from the compulsory attendance law which applied to all
minors up to their sixteenth birthday.   In the judgment
of the juvenile court the husband of the young lady was
to be held responsible for her attendance at school.

The Supreme Court upon appeal of the
case stated:

> The marriage relationship, regardless of the age of the
> persons involved, creates conditions and imposes obliga-
> tions upon the parties that are obviously inconsistent
> with compulsory school attendance or with either the
> husband or wife remaining under the legal control of
> parents or other persons.   Though young, the husband
> is none the less required to support his wife and family.
> The wife, in the event there should be a child in the
> family, could hardly be expected to attend school during
> the weeks preceding or following its birth.

Judge Kennon further answers those who argue that the
husband has control of his wife and, therefore, is responsible
for her school attendance: "No reasonable man, particularly
one who has been married for many years, would contend
that the husband . . . has 'control or charge' of his wife
in the manner formerly exercised by the parent or guardian."

The judgment of the juvenile court committing the relatrix
was annulled and the proceedings against her dismissed.

---

[14] State v. Priest, 210 La 389, 27 S(2d) 173 (1946).

Using information gleaned from the *Priest* case, the Supreme Court of Louisiana in 1949 again ruled that the compulsory school law was not applicable to a child emancipated by marriage. *In re State in Interest of Goodwin* the court reviewed the case of a young girl, fourteen years of age, who was placed in a detention home pending further investigation after preliminary charges of committing an act of juvenile delinquency-truancy.[15] She was released in the custody of a lady who said she would bring her back to the detention home later in the day after taking her to church.

During the afternoon, the child, giving her age as sixteen, married with the consent of her mother. The husband and wife lived together for a few days, and then she was returned to the detention home. Proceedings were instituted for the girl's release two days later. The judge of the juvenile court in a hearing to determine what was for the best interest of the child revealed her home situation was such as to place her in the position of being a neglected child of good moral character. She was prior to her marriage a regular attendant at church and until a few weeks before her marriage a regular attendant at school. The lower court ordered ". . . that this evidence disclosed she was, at the time the charge was made, a neglected child in that she was without proper guardianship and, as such, in need of the care and protection of the state in order that she might be prevented from assuming the duties and responsibilities of married life." She was ordered committed to the State Industrial School for Girls.

On appeal to the higher court the marriage was held valid, and the Supreme Court of Louisiana with respect to compulsory school attendance stated that the child was emancipated by marriage:

. . . although until she reaches the age of eighteen she is not relieved of all of the disabilities that attach to a minority by this emancipation, she is relieved of parental control and, as was held in the *Priest* case, is no longer

---

[15] In re State in Interest of Goodwin, 214 La 1062, 39 S(2d) 731 (1949).

amenable to the compulsory school attendance law of this state. Furthermore, having acquired the status of a wife, it is not only her right but also her duty to live with her husband at their matrimonial domicile and to follow him wherever he chooses to reside.

The Supreme Court of Louisiana further explained:

While we view with sympathy the trial judge's deep convictions of the tragedy inherent in the marriage of girls of tender years and his skepticism of any ultimate good resulting therefrom, we recognize the basic fact that under our system of government the matter of fixing the public policy of this state with respect to the age at which people may or may not marry as well as fixing the status of marriages solemnized in violation thereof lies exclusively within the province of the legislative branch.

The adoptive parents of an eleven-year-old girl took her and a young man to a football game out of state; and while they were there, the marriage of the couple was consented to and witnessed by the parents. Gans, the parent, was charged with acts which tend to contribute to the delinquency of a minor.[16] The Supreme Court of Ohio, in considering the circumstances to determine the guilt or innocence of Gans, based its decision largely upon the interference with the youth's education by the defendant and mentioned points concerning compulsory school attendance which heretofore were not emphasized by the courts. It was made clear by the court:

. . . that it is the duty of every parent to see that a child between 6 and 18 does in fact attend school unless excused therefrom for one or more of the reasons set out in the latter part of the statute. A close examination of those reasons fails to disclose that marital duties such as house cleaning, cooking, washing, caring for infants, etc., are among them.

---

16 State of Ohio v. Gans, 168 OhioSt 174, 151 NE(2d) 709 (1958).

The court held that non-compliance with the compulsory school attendance law was against the public policy of Ohio and further stated:

We do not mean to imply that a high school education provides a modern person with world-shaking tools of knowledge such as those of the scientists who work with atomic energy. It seems beyond argument to this court, however, that a child who is not *at least exposed* to his own potentialities by a high school education . . . can hardly be expected to realize his potential either to himself or his community, regardless of his basic or natural intelligence.

Judge Matthias continued:

Although the records in these cases are silent as to whether Kay's marital duties have yet caused her truancy, this court would be remiss in its duty if it shut its eyes to the facts that the duties of homemaker are strenuous, and that there is a certain propensity among young married couples to propagate, neither of which activities is conducive to regular attendance at school.

If the girl should remain in school, it was pointed out, a successful marriage could adversely affect the morals of her fellow classmates.

After being found guilty of contributing to the delinquency of a minor in Ohio Supreme Court, Carl Gans was denied a petition by the United States Supreme Court for a writ of certiorari to the Supreme Court of Ohio.[17]

In 1962, a court in New York was asked to determine whether a girl within the required ages for school attendance who had married was "a person in need of supervision" because of her failure to attend school.[18] Dorothy Jean Rogers, fifteen years old in October, 1962, resided with her husband since her marriage in July, 1962. She registered for classes in the fall of 1962; but when she was questioned

---

[17] Gans v. Ohio, 359 US 945, 3 LEd(2d) —, 79 SCt 722 (Ohio, 1959).
[18] In re Rogers, 234 NYS(2d) 172 (1962).

by school authorities in regard to her failure to attend school, she replied that she was a housewife and was not subject to the school attendance laws of the state. The New York law requiring school attendance of all children between the ages of seven and sixteen did not give marriage as an exception.

Judge Coon declared that under the circumstances the girl was not "a person in need of supervision." In explanation he stated:

> Times and the mores of people have changed since the Legislature first created compulsory education. It is doubtful that any thought was given then to the existence of a situation such as is now before the Court relative to school attendance.

> The unquestioned advantages of school attendance by minors below sixteen years of age must therefore be equated against the harmful effects, if any, of forcing the association of a married fifteen-year old female with school children of such young and impressionable ages, especially where the former is not disposed to attend the school. It seems to the Court that the issue goes to the health, safety and welfare of more than just this respondent.

> An analogy can be drawn to the cases which hold that children may be excluded from school unless they have first been vaccinated on the basis that the health and welfare of all the children are concerned. . . .

> It seems ludicrous indeed that a school district can, on one hand, exclude pupils for not having been vaccinated against a practically non-existent disease and, on the other hand, compel a married fifteen-year-old to attend school and associate with other fifteen-year-olds. . . .

§ 3.3 Authority of school boards to exclude married pupils from school attendance

School boards are given such discretionary authority and judgment as is necessary for the day-to-day operation of the schools. The obligation of the boards is to adopt only those resolutions concerning the efficient operation of the schools which are reasonable and which may not be considered arbitrary or capricious; however, consideration of that which is reasonable is in itself at times arbitrary. School boards throughout the nation, because they feel that not to act is to sanction early marriage, are attempting to curb the rising figures in the number of teenage marriages in their local communities by passing various restrictions to be imposed upon young married pupils. Many have taken the steps they feel are necessary—one of which is eliminating the young married person from the local school scene. However effective this may be:

> The public schools of the United States were organized to educate pupils between given ages. There is no statutory regulation against the attendance of married boys and girls, and a board of school control has no discretionary right to discriminate against married pupils within the prescribed age limit by refusing them admittance to the public schools.[19]

In the case of *Nutt* v. *Board of Education of Goodland* the young lady in question was enrolled in the high school during the 1927-28 school year; but upon the successful completion of her work during the first semester, she left school.[20] At the beginning of the 1928-29 school year, she again enrolled in the high school and attended only one day after which she was informed by the school authorities that she would not be permitted to remain in school because she was married.

Dorothy Nutt married Oliver Mitchell in February, 1928; but she had lived with her husband for only a short time. Her baby was born August 9, 1928, not prematurely. It was stated in the proceedings that she had attended a school in a nearby town after separation from her husband, that while in attendance there she had been seen in the company of men other than her husband, and that she had

---

[19] John Messick, *The Discretionary Powers of School Boards* (Durham, North Carolina: Duke University Press, 1949), p. 102.

[20] Nutt v. Board of Education of Goodland, 128 Kan 507, 278 Pac 1065 (1929).

persuaded a sixteen-year-old girl to accompany her to a dance. Evidence was presented to the court that one of the young men with whom she had been seen was a cousin while another had offered her a ride home from school. The fact was also stated in court that Dorothy's mother had accompanied the two girls to the dance and that the other girl who was mentioned had the permission of her parents to attend the dance.

Affidavits in behalf of Dorothy Nutt were presented testifying that she was of good moral character and deportment, that she was a regular attendant at school before her withdrawal, and that she possessed a good reputation in general. The principal of the school in which she had been in attendance verified the statement that her character could not be questioned.

The Supreme Court of Kansas, ruling that a minor was entitled to an education in the public schools and could not be excluded solely on the basis of marital status, stated:

> The public schools are for the benefit of children within school age, and efficiency ought to be the sole object of those charged with the power and privilege of managing and conducting the same, and while great care should be taken to preserve order and proper discipline, it is proper also to see that no one within school age should be denied the privilege of attending school unless it is clear that the public interest demands the expulsion of such pupils or a denial of his right to attend. On the record submitted here, we are of the opinion the evidence was insufficient to warrant the board in excluding plaintiff's daughter from the schools of Goodland. It is the policy of the state to encourage the student to equip himself with a good education.

Insufficient evidence against the plaintiff's daughter justified her reinstatement in school. The court declared the young lady's desire to attend school indicative of character ". . . warranting favorable consideration" and that she should not be prevented ". . . from gaining an education which would better fit her to meet the problems of life."

In the same year the Supreme Court of Mississippi in *McLeod* v. *State* called the resolution adopted by the school trustees of Moss Point arbitrary and unreasonable by virtue of the fact that it prohibited married persons, although eligible in all other respects, from attendance at school.[21] Wanda Myers married between the age of fifteen and sixteen but was otherwise eligible for school attendance. She made application and was enrolled in the high school for the 1928-29 school session; however, before the opening date of school the superintendent, discovering that she was married, refused her admittance.

The Supreme Court of Mississippi stated that although it had been argued:

> . . . that marriage emancipates a child from all parental control of its conduct, as well as such control by the school authorities; and that the marriage relation brings about views of life which should not be known to unmarried children; that a married child in the public schools will make known to its associates in school such views, which will therefore be detrimental to the welfare of the school.

The court was unable "to appreciate the force of the argument"; and furthermore, it stated:

> Marriage is a domestic relation highly favored by law. When the relation is entered into with correct motives, the effect on husband and wife is refining and elevating, rather than demoralizing. Pupils associating in school with a child occupying such a relation, it seems, would be benefited instead of harmed.

The court, declaring the rule adopted by the school board unreasonable and arbitrary, commented that for married persons of school age to wish to continue their education and thereby become better qualified to meet the various problems of life was commendable and that they, as members of a student body ". . . are as much

---

[21] McLeod v. Mississippi ex rel. Colmer, 154 Miss 468, 122 So 737 (1929).

subject to the rules of school as unmarried people, and punishable to the same extent for a breach of such rules."

Almost thirty years later, in 1957, the Supreme Court of Tennessee upheld a regulation of the Marion County School Board, *State ex rel. Thompson* v. *Marion County Board of Education,* that pupils who married during the school year would be automatically "expelled" for the remainder of that current school term and that those pupils who married during the summer vacation would not be allowed to attend school the next succeeding term.[22] Indicating that teenage marriages in the various high schools of the county were detrimental to the operation of the schools, the Marion County School Board in November, 1955, adopted the above mentioned resolution and made its adoption known to the pupils in each of the high schools in the county. The action taken by the board of education resulted from the requests of four principals who felt that there had been "a deterioration of the discipline and decorum in the schools" caused by student marriages. The principals, considered experts by the court, maintained that confusion and disorder ". . . mostly occur immediately after the marriage and during the period of readjustment, and the influence of married students on the other students is also greatest at this time."

A young lady in her fourth year of attendance in the high school at Jasper married, and was forbade the privilege of attendance at school for the remainder of the term. She was told, however, that in view of the board rules, she could re-enter the next year. The father-in-law of the student sought by writ of mandamus to compel the school officials to restore the girl to attendance at the high school.

The Supreme Court of Tennessee, basing its decision upon the testimony of the "experts" who declared that the attendance of students for a few months immediately following their marriage had a detrimental effect upon the efficient operation and well-being of the school, declared the resolution adopted by the board within the exercise of their power

---

[22] Tennessee ex rel. Thompson v. Marion County Board of Education, 202 Tenn 29, 302 SW(2d) 57 (1957).

and reasonable. In rendering the judgment for the court, Justice Tomlinson said:

We are accustomed to accept the testimony of experts in the various fields of human activity as to what is reasonably necessary for the welfare of the particular activity as to which this expert therein is testifying. No reason is suggested as to why this practice should not be followed when the witness is an expert in the field of operating public high schools. Certainly the principals of the high schools in question should be regarded by reason of training, experience and observation as possessing particular knowledge as to the problem which they say is made by the marriage and uninterrupted attendance of students in their respective schools.

The court further stated:

Boards of Education, rather than courts, are charged with the important and difficult duty of operating the public schools. So, it is not a question of whether this or that individual judge or court considers a given regulation adopted by the Board as expedient. The Court's duty, regardless of personal views, is to uphold the Board's regulation unless it is generally viewed as being arbitrary and unreasonable. Any other policy would result in confusion detrimental to the progress and efficiency of our public school system.

In formulating policies concerning married students, school officials often give consideration to any special provisions which should be made for pregnant students. The Trenton Board of Education adopted such a resolution which provided for the withdrawal from school of any student upon the knowledge of pregnancy and for the school officials to require a doctor's examination in cases of question. The resolution, which was enacted in February, 1961, was challenged in *Ohio ex rel. Idle v. Chamberlain* as being unreasonable and beyond the power delegated to boards of education.[23] The court proceedings showed

_____

23 Ohio ex rel. Idle v. Chamberlain, 175 NE(2d) 539 (CP Ohio, 1961).

that Linda Idle was an excellent student, had continued her school work at home after her withdrawal, and would be permitted to return to school in the fall of 1961 after the birth of her child.

The common pleas court of Ohio ruled that an attempt to prohibit a student from school attendance solely on the basis of marital status would be against the public policy of Ohio, but:

> The evidence here shows that the relator's further school attendance was denied in the interest of her physical well-being and not as a punitive measure. Furthermore, is it unreasonable for a Board, having in mind that it serves the entire student body, to consider the effect upon the other students the continued presence in the classroom of a pregnant fellow student might have? May it not calculate that such presence might adversely affect the morale of the student body, cause disruption to the orderly operation of the school's daily activities and to some extent, interfere with the discipline and government of the students?

> We think the Board may make such evaluations and having come to a conclusion in respect thereto and incorporated the same in the adoption of a policy and regulation, a Court cannot and should not label it as constituting an abuse of discretion.

§ 3.4 Authority of school boards to exclude married pupils from participation in extracurricular activities

Although litigation has been limited, courts thus far have agreed that boards of education are without authority to exclude pupils permanently from school attendance solely on the basis of marital status. Some school boards, no longer able to bar married pupils legally from attendance at school, have sought other methods which they felt might discourage marriages among the student body. In the absence of any statute concerning the participation of married pupils in the school program, some school officials, by virtue of the discretionary authority vested in them, have attempted to restrict the school activities of those who marry by confining their participation solely to classroom work and by barring them from participation in extracurricular activities. If the question of legality of such control should arise, one would be wise to review four cases which have come before the courts.

The Garland Independent School District was upheld by the Court of Civil Appeals of Texas, *Kissick v. Garland Independent School Dist.*, in its resolution ". . . providing that married students or previously married students should be restricted wholly to classroom work and barring them from participation in athletic or other exhibitions and prohibiting them from holding class offices or other positions of honor other than academic honors such as valedictorian and salutatorian."[24] The court declared that the resolution was neither capricious, discriminatory, nor unreasonable as applied to the case of Jerry Kissick.

Jerry Kissick, who had been a letterman on the football team of 1958-59, married in March, 1959. The boy continued in school after his marriage, but he was barred from further participation in athletic activities. The young man in question stated that he planned to play football in high school the next year in looking to college and an athletic scholarship.

The record presented in court showed that the resolution was passed after an "extensive study" by the local parent-teacher association which showed the ill effects of married students participating in extracurricular activities with unmarried students. That there had been an alarming increase in juvenile marriages in the Garland school was brought out in the hearing.

A professional psychologist, who was also a board member, gave results of a survey which he had conducted as indicative of the need for such a resolution. In a postal card poll of the parents of young people of junior and senior high school age, the vote was nine to one favoring a resolution

---

[24] Kissick v. Garland Independent School Dist., 330 SW(2d) 708 (Tex, 1959).

limiting participation of married students to classroom activities. The psychologist said:

. . . that problems existing in connection with married students participating in school activities such as overnight athletic trips, band trips, etc., was detrimental to the efficiency of the system; that in the District last year (1958) there was a total of sixty-two married students; of these twenty-four students had dropped out of school, and of the remainder, at least one-half experienced a drop of at least ten points in grades; the study further demonstrated a conflict in the general diffusion of knowledge "as witnessed by the drop in grades and lack of opportunity to teach some of them because of their actual dropping out of school."

Since the board's action to discourage teenage marriages in a community that was vexed by the problem was not considered arbitrary and unreasonable, all points of appeal upon consideration were overruled; and the judgment of the trial court was affirmed, further supporting the legal principle that school boards have the power to take action which will expedite the efficient operation of the public schools as long as the action is not arbitrary, capricious, or unreasonable.

A writ of mandamus was sought by the plaintiffs in *Cochrane* v. *Board of Education of Mesick Consol. School Dist.* to compel the school authorities to permit Ronald Cochrane and David Shively to play football regardless of their marital status.[25] Upon appeal by the plaintiff from an adverse decision of the lower court, the attorney general of the state intervened; and the appellant and intervenor stated:

It is submitted by the Attorney General that the action of the school board, in taking what it frankly admits is punitive action, designed to humiliate and ridicule the plaintiff students before their classmates so as to dis-

---

[25] Cochrane v. Board of Education of Mesick Consol. School Dist., **360** Mich 390, 103 NW(2d) 569 (1960).

courage other marriages, is violating the public policy
of the state by attacking the married status of these
students as "wrongdoing", and that the rule in question
is clearly void for that reason alone. The concern of
the law is to protect, not to attack, the state of matrimony,
and to exalt, not to undermine, the security of legal
marriages . . . they are entitled, by law and public
policy, to the respect and security of community acceptance in their married status, as well as to all the benefits
of equal access to all public educational facilities, including their earned status in the co-curricular activities.
To deprive them of the intangible security of their pride
of achievement in the "glamour" titles and offices so
important to the high school student, at a time of life
when they are peculiarly sensitive to acceptance and
approval by their contemporaries, is to interfere not only
with their education but also with their marriages, by
undermining their morale in this respect, thus condemning
their marital status through the exclusionary rule . . .
instead of making the status of marriage itself an occasion for stripping students of achievement and rank, so
as to deprive them of the admiration of fellow students,
it is the duty of the school board to respect and exalt the
status of matrimony . . . if, however, the community
is to take a position against high school marriages, the
way to do it is through legislation . . . not through
school board interference with the prerogative of the legislature, the parents, and the church.

In spite of the opinion expressed by the attorney general,
the Supreme Court of Michigan affirmed the position of the
school board; but it was a divided court which said ". . .
that the school district did not violate the statute guaran-
teeing to all students an equal right to public educational
facilities by excluding the students from participation in
co-curricular activities."

David Shively, married July 27, 1958, and Ronald Cochrane, married August 17, 1958, and their fathers had filed
for a writ to reinstate the boys in the co-curricular activities
from which they had been excluded because of their marri-

ages. Participation had been denied the boys in compliance with the resolution adopted August 28, 1958, stating that "married students attending schools shall not be eligible to participate in any co-curricular activities; i.e., competitive sports, band, glee club, class and club officers, cheer leading, physical education, class plays and etc." The resolution which was passed after the marriage of both boys was upheld by a trial court and was sustained by the Michigan Supreme Court. Four justices of the Supreme Court expressed opposition to the resolution finding it unreasonable and arbitrary and stating that evidence was not presented which would indicate that the marriages of the boys would have ill effects upon the administration of the school in any way. Three of the justices affirmed the decision of the lower court in their belief that the resolution was reasonable and enacted within the power of the board; the eighth justice affirmed the decision of the lower court on the grounds that the question was moot since the boy in question had been graduated.

Since the *Cochrane* case, *supra*, in 1960, two additional opportunities have been presented in which one may observe the courts' rulings concerning participation of married young men in the athletic program of the public high schools in which they were in attendance. In *Ohio ex rel. Baker* v. *Stevenson* the plaintiff questioned the validity of the school rule which prohibited married students from participation in extracurricular activities and therein precluded Michael Baker, a married student, from playing basketball.[26] The rule was attacked as being arbitrary, unreasonable, discriminatory, and against the public policy of the state in that it penalized marriage.

The pupil bringing the case prior to his marriage had been active in extracurricular activities, had served as co-captain of the basketball team, and was recognized as an outstanding member of the team. The claim was made that the boy was popular with other students and with the teachers and that he had never been a disciplinary problem.

---

[26] Ohio ex rel. Baker v. Stevenson, 189 NE(2d) 181 (CP Ohio, 1962).

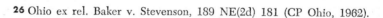

Evidence was submitted to the court to show that high school marriages had become a problem to the local authorities. The local school authorities, concerned with the high drop-out rate of pupils who married, adopted the rule upon the recommendation of various groups and individuals who studied the "moral problem" as it appeared in the high schools of the city.

The court of common pleas of Ohio reasoned:

It is a matter of common knowledge that the student who excels in athletics sets a pattern of conduct which his associates in the school are proud to follow. The "hero", in the eyes of his followers, "can do no wrong."

. . . We have all witnessed the effect upon the entire student body caused when the "star" football or basketball player decides to adopt a manner of speech, type of haircut, wear a particular kind of clothing, eat a particular kind of food, expresses a preference for a definite song, singer, playing record, actor, performer and ad infinitum.

❋   ❋   ❋

Students today are, of course, more ready to accept the actions of their peers as the thing to do. If any married students are in a position of idolization, the more desirous is the group to mimic.

Since evidence presented on behalf of the school board indicated that the rule had been promulgated only after deliberation and in the best interest of all pupils, the court declared the rule valid as applied and further stated: "Any policy which is directed toward making juvenile marriages unpopular and to be avoided should have the general public's whole-hearted approval and support."

The Supreme Court of Utah, a few months later, told a married pupil, *Starkey* v. *Board of Education of Davis County School Dist.*, that the school rule which permitted pupils already married to participate in extracurricular activities but barred pupils marrying after the adoption of the regulation from such participation was within the authority of school officials to enforce.[27] The court, recog-

---

[27] Starkey v. Board of Education of Davis County School Dist., 381 P(2d) 718 (Utah, 1963).

nizing that large numbers of pupils drop out of school before finishing high school and that pupils who marry accept additional responsibilities not conducive to finishing school, pointed out to the plaintiff that he had a constitutional right to attend school and to get married as he claimed. The court continued: "But he has no 'right' to compel the Board of Education to exercise its discretion to his personal advantage so he can participate in the named activities."

§ 3.5 Summary

There is no doubt that boards of education have the legal authority to adopt such rules and regulations for the efficient operation of the public schools as are reasonable and necessary and not in conflict with the constitution or existing statutes. In the past several years, however, school boards have been questioned in instances as to the reasonableness of certain courses of action which they have taken. Particularly is this true in the case of their dealing with married pupils in the public schools.

School boards in an attempt to stem the increasing number of high school marriages in their communities have considered and adopted resolutions which would fall mainly in three categories: attempts to compel married pupils to attend school; attempts to expel or suspend married pupils from school; and attempts to exclude married pupils from participation in extracurricular activities. Litigation declaring the usurpation of rights of the individuals concerned has been instituted against boards of education and in eleven instances in the past thirty-three years has reached the appellate courts. The courts, in general, have declared that the operation and management of the schools is important and should be left to the discretion of school boards except in the case where their action proves to be unreasonable, arbitrary, and capricious.

In the cases of *State* v. *Priest, supra,* n 14 and *In re State in Interest of Goodwin, supra,* n 15, the courts declared the action taken by school districts to compel married students to attend school unreasonable. They stated that children who married took upon themselves certain obligations which were not conducive to school attendance, and therefore, were not amenable to the compulsory school law. A few years later the Supreme Court of Ohio in *Ohio* v. *Gans, supra,* n 16, found a parent guilty of contributing to the delinquency of a minor because he had given his consent and permitted a marriage which would in itself make his daughter a delinquent if she were remiss in school attendance. The parent upon appeal to the United States Supreme Court, *Gans* v. *Ohio, supra,* n 17, was denied a writ of certiorari which would have resulted in an opportunity to change the judgment rendered by the state court. Another case concerning the authority of school officials to compel married pupils to attend school may be found in *In re Rogers, supra,* n 18. The judge in this case found the married minor not in need of supervision and emphasized the possible ill effects upon other pupils if she were required to attend school.

When school boards attempted to discourage teenage marriages by denying school attendance to married students, the courts again held the actions of such school boards unreasonable and a denial of the guaranteed right of the child of school age to attend the public schools. In the case of *Nutt* v. *Board of Education of Goodland, supra,* n 20, and again in *McLeod* v. *Mississippi ex rel. Colmer, supra,* n 21, the courts declared the desire of the young people to continue their educations commendable and attempts to prevent them from so doing on the sole basis of marital status unreasonable.

Almost thirty years later the Supreme Court of Tennessee upheld the resolution of Marion county school board, *Tennessee ex rel. Thompson* v. *Marion County Board of* *Education, supra,* n 22, to bar students from attending school in the term following their marriage. The board of education presented sufficient evidence to warrant the decision that for a period of time immediately following teenage marriage, the normal activities of the school were impaired due to confusion created by the marriage.

The common pleas court of Ohio ruled in *Ohio ex rel. Idle* v. *Chamberlain, supra,* n 23, that the board was justified in suspending a married student who was pregnant. The board's action was upheld on the basis that the decision had been made to protect the health of the pregnant student and to guard the welfare of the student body.

On the basis that participation in extracurricular activities by married students was detrimental to the welfare of other children and, therefore, to the efficient operation of the school, other school boards have ruled that married students should not be permitted to participate in extracurricular activities. The decision of the trial court was affirmed by the Court of Civil Appeals of Texas in the case of *Kissick* v. *Garland Independent School Dist., supra,* n 24. The court ruled that the board was neither arbitrary nor unreasonable in its action taken which excluded Jerry Kissick from participation in football the school year after his marriage although he was looking to football in hopes of receiving an athletic scholarship to college.

In *Cochrane* v. *Board of Education of Mesick Consolidated School Dist., supra,* n. 25, the Supreme Court of Michigan rendered a decision, although the justices were not in agreement, that a resolution limiting the participation of married students wholly to classroom activity was within the power of the board and not arbitrary, capricious, or unreasonable. Since the decision of the court was divisive, 4-1-3, there remained some doubt as to what future rulings on the legality of such resolutions might be, but within three years two other cases, *Ohio ex rel. Baker* v. *Stevenson, supra,* n 26, and *Starkey* v. *Board of Education of Davis County School Dist., supra,* n 27, were brought to court. In both instances of litigation the decision rendered was in favor of the school board in that evidence was presented to show that the rule in question was promulgated and enforced out of concern for the welfare of the student body.

In each instance concerning participation of married pupils in extracurricular activities, the court took care to state that the rule as applied in that particular case could be considered valid and that other stipulations, specifications, or restrictions in the rule were not being weighed. It remains to be seen whether school boards can legally limit participation of pupils in any activity of the school solely on the basis of marital status.

The decisions made in the instances of litigation thus far introduced exemplify the judgment of the courts concerning the legality of certain resolutions which attempt to regulate high school marriages. It would be well for those individuals who are charged with the responsibility of operating the schools and who feel that high school marriages in their community are detrimental to the government and discipline of the schools and, therefore, have created a need for regulations by boards of control to consider not only their local situations but the legal aspects involved in their actions.

Chapter 4

EXTENT TO WHICH SCHOOL OFFICIALS MAY LEGALLY REGULATE THE DRESS AND PERSONAL APPEARANCE OF PUPILS

Section
4.1   Attempts to regulate dress through planned programs
4.2   Authority of school officials to prescribe certain types of dress
4.3   Authority of school officials to prohibit certain types of dress
4.4   Summary

Educators and laymen alike who read the current periodicals regularly have encountered articles which decry the unconventionality in the grooming and dress of the "younger" generation. Many accounts which describe the action taken by administrators in attempting to regulate the dress of young people in their charges have appeared in recent publications. The instances which made the headlines usually did so by virtue of the extreme apparel involved or the unusual action taken. School officials in prescribing apparel that is appropriate for school wear are often fraught with the problems of determining just when a pupil's attire, haircut or hairstyle, or make-up becomes extreme, unconventional, and disturbing to the decorum of the school.

Few adults of today have difficulty in recalling their experiences following World War I when "bobbed" hair for women became the subject for a nationwide controversy, a controversy which was resolved in a few years by the acceptance of the hair-style as being attractive, neat, and in good taste. Others will recall upon reflection the furor encountered when young women came to school dressed "improperly" in slacks; the attitudes that condemned were altered when employment in war plants necessitated such dress. Those who have lived many decades have noted similar controversies generated by bustles, "stockingless legs," split skirts, and chignons. Through the years many of the most staunch adversaries have surrendered to the changing mode of dress and have themselves partaken. Today, the "beehive" and bouffant hair-styles for young

70

women, the long hair, sideburns, or shaved heads for young men, low-slung trousers, boots, and black leather jackets are creating disturbances similar to those in earlier decades.

§ 4.1 Attempts to regulate dress through planned programs

Few individuals would challenge the authority of school officials to regulate the dress of pupils when it becomes so extreme as to cause an obvious disruption of the discipline of the school and thereby interfere with the efficient operation and management of the school in attempting to achieve its educational goals.   Seldom, if ever, have many young people who have gone to such an extreme in their personal appearance revolted against disciplinary action when their offenses have been discussed and the consequences of their actions explained.   As those who work with young people relate their observations pertaining to the personal appearance of pupils, they find the nature of their problems is similar; and diversity is found only in the details.

To find those who adhere to the belief that the personality and motives of an individual are reflected in his dress is not difficult.   It has been apparent to some who have worked with children considered delinquent ". . . that certain styles of dress have become identified with hoodlumism in the minds of police, educators, and citizens generally."[1]   Reasoning further that a change in habits of dress may eliminate some cases of vandalism, inappropriate talk and behavior, and delinquency in general, some school authorities have encouraged campaigns of various kinds which are planned to improve the personal appearance of members of the student body.

Handel, who was the principal of a junior high school, felt that an informal atmosphere in his school created conditions which led to undesirable behavior and fads.[2]   Most

----

[1] Joseph Manch, "Effective Ways of Regulating Student Dress," The Bulletin of The National Association of Secondary School Principals, XLI (April, 1957), p. 144.

[2] Harvey Handel, "Can We Outlaw Fad Clothing?" School Executive LXVII (November, 1957), pp. 68 to 69.

offenders of order who were sent to his office for disciplinary action were, Handel noted, members of the "black-jacket mob" which was recognized by the police, parents, teachers, classmates, and younger children as a potential threat to a peaceful atmosphere. Not only had the jackets worn by the group become symbols for anti-social behavior, but younger children wishing to acquire the "gang" status had adopted the same type of clothing. When residents of the school community began to express their displeasure at the behavior of these gang members, Handel sent a letter to the parents of each pupil in the student body stating that dungarees, engineers' boots, black leather jackets, and sideburns were inappropriate dress for school. A few pupils, reluctant to accept Handel's suggestion, were taken home to change their clothes; and of the 700 students enrolled, only three parents expressed disapproval to the principal for the action he had taken. Since taking a stand against the clothing which was alleged to have been a symbol of undesirable behavior, Handel says there has been less boisterous behavior and less vandalism in the school.

Operating on the premise that improved dress would improve behavior, Manch, associate superintendent for school-community coordination in the Buffalo public schools, enlisted the aid of the "Inter-High School Student Council," which is composed of representatives from fourteen public high schools in Buffalo.[3] When asked to make recommendations concerning the appropriate dress for pupils, the council submitted proposals which included clothes which were inexpensive, comfortable, and practical. At the same time the representatives from the schools discouraged pupils from wearing dungarees, T-shirts, sweat shirts, V-neck sweaters without blouses, shorts, party dresses, slacks, extreme shoe styles, and ornate jewelry. Special assembly programs were held to present the proposals to other pupils, and publicity for the "dress-right program" was furnished by the local press.

Arnstein reported in an article written later that fourteen principals two years after the program in Buffalo was

---

[3] Manch, "Effective Ways of Regulating Student Dress," pp. 144 to 145.

inaugurated indicated that there had been an improvement in the dress of the pupils and that ten of the principals attributed the improved dress to the program.[4] Thirteen of the principals believed that there was a positive correlation between dress and behavior, and all fourteen principals recommended that the "dress-right" program be continued.

Many schools throughout the country have been successful in attacking inappropriate dress by adopting programs planned cooperatively by pupils, faculty members, and parents. In other schools personal appearance which has been consistently, or persistently, inappropriate has been dealt with through [parent-principal conferences or, in extreme cases, through suspension or expulsion.] Because they feel that the matter of pupil dress should be left to the discretion of parents, because they fear that they do not have the legal support to regulate pupil dress, or because they are afraid of what may result as a consequence of attempted regulation, some school authorities have refused to take action of any sort regarding the personal appearance of pupils.

Not the least of the problems associated with dress to confront school officials is the problem which arises from a pupil's refusal to wear the prescribed attire for a particular school activity such as band, shop, home economics, or physical education. Perhaps an example familiar to most educators will be found in the objections originating from apparel required for physical education. Pupils who refuse to "dress out" many times give reasons of a personal nature such as religious convictions, modesty, or lack of proper attire. Frustrated not only by the pupil's refusal to obey instructions and the reasons given but also by the effect the action may have upon the discipline of the class, teachers or principals respond in various ways: some let the person dress in a manner consistent with his belief or his wardrobe; some excuse the person from participation in the activity; some exclude the person from the class or school; and some devise various penalties for not "dressing out."

---

[4] George Arnstein, "Students Vote on Student Dress," The Clearing House, XXXII (March, 1958), pp. 387 to 389.

Whatever the problems may be concerning the regulation of pupil dress and personal appearance, most administrators have found it necessary to consider the problems and to determine the position they will take. Their determination has relied heavily upon personal background and community custom. The number of discussions heard and the number of articles appearing in the daily newspapers pertaining to the regulation of pupil dress when compared to the number of instances of litigation would give an indication that many of the daily conflicts which arise from problems related to personal appearance and dress are resolved in some manner satisfactory to the affected parties.

§ 4.2 Authority of school officials to prescribe certain types of dress

Although certain modes of dress may be universally acceptable or unacceptable at one point in history, a lapse of a few years may reverse the position of society regarding personal appearance. Many school authorities express a reluctance in attempting to regulate pupil dress and give as a reason, if no other, the fear of action which may result from their attempts and which may reflect upon the local school staff and the teaching profession itself. Expressing the belief that the development of habits of proper dress is another of the responsibilities of educators and feeling that unconventional dress is a detriment to school discipline, other school officers and administrators place restrictions upon the wearing apparel of pupils which they deem necessary to the efficient operation of the school. Unable to rely upon statutes prescribing the appropriate attire for school wear, school authorities, if they are to take prudent action in their attempts to regulate pupil dress, must consider not only the changing customs and the underlying reasons for unusual dress or appearance; but they also must give consideration to the legal angle of the controls which they are contemplating.

J. C. McCaskill attacked as unconstitutional the regulation which required that all male pupils who were over "four feet and six inches" tall and who were between certain ages must wear a prescribed uniform in order to attend a public school in Bainbridge, Georgia.[5]   Upon considering the case wherein McCaskill sought to restrain the superintendent and trustees of the public schools of Bainbridge from refusing his sons admission to school for not complying with the rule, the superior court of Decatur County refused the injunction sought upon the ground that the school officials were within their authority when they passed the rule in question.   The plaintiffs appealed to Supreme Court of Georgia which affirmed the judgment in the main bill and dismissed the cross-bill on the grounds that the plaintiffs had chosen improper legal remedy to restrain enforcement of the rule and that there had been no allegation that the rule had been enforced.   The court in discussing the absence of allegation concerning enforcement of the rule said, "No principle is more clearly recognized than that equity will not attempt to do a thing which is vain; and it would be useless indeed to grant relief before injury is even threatened."

The Supreme Court of Oklahoma in *Connell* v. *Gray* was asked to consider a case where a pupil had been denied admission to Oklahoma Agricultural and Mechanical College for non-payment of term fees which include a deposit for clothing and equipment to be used in the gymnasium.[6] The court modified a lower court order in favor of Ruth Gray by saying:

If there is no appropriate fund available for the replacing of broken vessels or apparatus in the laboratory, or for the support of the gymnasium or the athletic association, or for the publication of the college magazine, or for the repair of the musical instruments and the typewriting machines, then, as to such students in their course of study and training that use the laboratory or the gymnasium or the magazine, or participate in the athletic association, within their college course, a reasonable incidental fee may be required after admission. . . . To require the supplying of the required uniform as a

5 McCaskill v. Bower, 126 Ga 341, 54 SE 942 (1906).
6 Connell v. Gray, 33 Okla 591, 127 Pac 417 (1912).

condition precedent to entrance comes also within the same rule; but, if the proposed student has supplied himself with such uniform, then there is no necessity for a deposit for such purpose.

Perhaps a more widely known case concerning the prescription of uniforms by school authorities is *Jones v. Day.*[7] The father of Ben Shaifer Jones instituted proceedings in behalf of his minor son against the superintendent and the trustees of Wilkinson County. Jones sought to enjoin the enforcement of a resolution concerning uniforms and to have the resolution declared null and void. In September, 1918, the board of trustees had enacted a resolution requiring high school boys to wear khaki uniforms and ordered the principal to enforce the regulation on all pupils in public places within five miles of the school every day including Saturday and Sunday. The Supreme Court of Mississippi ruled that since certain pupils were boarding pupils at Wilkinson County Agricultural High School, they were under the care and custody of school authorities during the entire school term; and the rule, therefore, was applicable to them ". . . until they cease to be under the care and control of the school management . . ."; but the court added that the rule in being applied to day pupils could be in effect only when the pupils were under the care and control of the school and not in parental charge. In explanation the court emphasized that children were considered under the control of parents except while going to and from school and while in school.

Of the six girls in the graduating class of Casey High School, three girls were not granted a diploma or seated on the platform during the graduation exercises because of their refusal to wear gowns which had an offensive odor.[8] The plaintiff had complied with the rules and regulations and made above the passing grade during her four years of attendance at the high school; but when she requested

---

[7] Jones v. Day, 127 Miss 136, 89 So 906 (1921).

[8] Valentine v. Independent School Dist. of Casey, 187 Iowa 555, 174 NW 334 (1919); 191 Iowa 1100, 184 NW 434 (1921).

grades from the superintendent of the public schools, he denied her request, ". . . . claiming that the said grades were his private property, and that plaintiff, nor any one for her, could have said grades nor access to same."[9]

The Supreme Court of Iowa in granting a writ of mandamus to compel the issuance of a diploma and grades declared the action of school authorities unreasonable, arbitrary, and in excess of their power saying:

> . . . even without a statute, there is an implied legal duty on the part of such officers to issue written evidence on the plaintiff's graduation in the form of a certificate, a diploma, or the like, to those who have satisfactorily completed the prescribed course of study, unless for sufficient reasons they are justified in withholding it.

Two years later the Supreme Court of Iowa was again asked to review the circumstances of the Valentine incident.[10] Although the school authorities presented additional reasons why the diploma should not be granted, the court refused to place any emphasis upon this justification since it seemed apparent that the reasons had no "causal" relation to the board's refusal to grant the diploma in question on the evening of graduation exercises and that if it had not been for the gown episode, the diploma would have been issued. The delivery of a diploma to a pupil who had completed the prescribed course of study was declared by the court a ministerial act. Declaring unreasonable a rule which provides for withholding a diploma for refusal to wear a cap and gown, the court said:

> The wearing of a cap and gown on commencement night has no relation to educational values, the discipline of the school, scholastic grades, or intellectual advancement. Such a rule may be justified in some instances from the viewpoint of economy, but from a legal viewpoint the board might as well attempt to direct the wearing of overalls by the boys and calico dresses by the girls.

---

9 Id at 187 Iowa 555, 174 NW 334 (1919).
10 Id at 191 Iowa 1100, 183 NW 334 (1921).

The enforcement of such a rule is purely arbitrary and especially so when the offending pupil has been passed for graduation after the performance on her part of all prescribed educational requirements. We are not questioning the wearing of caps and gowns. It is a custom we approve. (The board may deny the right of a graduate to participate in the public ceremony of graduation unless a cap and gown is worn.\

The Supreme Court of Iowa further ruled that the granting of a diploma to a pupil who had satisfactorily completed the prescribed courses and who had otherwise qualified was mandatory and pointed out that ". . . although such duty is not expressly enjoined upon the board by statute, it does arise by necessary and reasonable implication."

In its judgment favoring Valentine the court said:

This plaintiff, having accepted the benefits of education tendered by the public school system established in the independent school district of Casey, and having complied with all the rules and regulations precedent to graduation may not be denied her diploma by the arbitrary action of the school board subsequent to her being made the recipient of the honors of graduation. It is also clear that plaintiff is entitled to a certificate of her grades.

A divided court dismissed the action brought by Julian Lamme, *Colorado ex rel. Lamme* v. *Buckland*, against the school committee that had expelled his daughter from a public school for her refusal to comply with the rules and regulations which designated uniforms to be worn by girls.[11] The Supreme Court of Colorado, considering the record of the lower court, was unable to determine the reason for the lower court's action quashing a writ of mandamus sought by the plaintiff. Whether the judgment of the lower court had rested on the ground that the adoption and enforcement of a rule requiring uniforms for girls attending

---

[11] Colorado ex rel. Lamme v. Buckland, 84 Colo 240, 269 Pac 15 (1928).

a public school was a reasonable exercise of the power which had been vested in the school committee by the legislature or whether the court's decision to dismiss the petition was based upon the ground that the relator had not used the proper procedure designated in the statutes for the redress of grievances concerning rules and regulations adopted by schools was not evident in the records presented.

Regardless of the reasons underlying the action of the lower court, the Supreme Court of Colorado explained that the legal remedy for those aggrieved by a rule of the school board could be found in an appeal through the proper channels provided by the statutes of Colorado which included an appeal to the local superintendent of schools and the state board of education. The court indicated that only after exhausting the statutory remedy could the aggrieved person be entitled to present his question to the courts for consideration. The court further reasoned that the legislature, in providing a legal remedy, ". . . clearly indicates a purpose to vest in the school authorities the adjustment and settlement of such controversies." A dissenting judge expressed the opinion that the question should be heard by the court; and a second judge, concurring specially, disagreed with the reason given for affirmance by the majority because he felt that the writ should have been quashed on the basis that the rule was valid and not shown to be unreasonable.

The courts in recent years seldom have been asked to pass upon the validity and reasonableness of a school rule requiring pupils to wear a uniform to the public schools since it is a rarity to find such a rule in existence. To encounter complaints from pupils or parents who object to certain types of attire prescribed by school officials or teachers for particular courses, however, has not been unusual or rare. The first case dealing with prescribed clothing for physical education that has been reported by the higher courts may be found in Alabama, *Mitchell* v. *McCall*, where Eulene Mitchell was suspended from high school for refusing to participate in a required physical edu-

cation class.[12]   Her refusal to take part in the class was
based upon her objection to the costume which was to be
worn for the gymnastic exercises.   Her contention that the
costume was "immodest and sinful" was supplemented by
her objection to being in the presence of the teacher and
the other pupils who wore the costume.   The plaintiff
voiced the opinion that required participation and presence
in such a class violated his religious beliefs and those of
his daughter guaranteed by the First and Fourteenth Amend-
ments of the Constitution of the United States.

When the complaint reached the school authorities, the
plaintiff was told that the girl would be permitted to
dress in a manner which she considered suitable and would
not be required to take any exercises which she or her
parents thought were immodest in the clothing that she
chose.   Mitchell, not appeased by the concessions made
to his daughter by the school, expressed his objection to
his daughter's being in the presence of others dressed in
the manner described; and for this reason he sought satisfaction through the courts.   The Supreme Court of Alabama
pointed out that: (1) reasonable concessions to the girl
had been made by the school; (2) attendance in schools
in Alabama was voluntary; (3) the state constitution required physical education for pupils attending the public
schools; and (4) the appellant was in an all girl class.   In
answer to the appellant's contention that his daughter
should be placed in a special class which conformed to
her religious beliefs and in which she would not stand
out as a "speckled bird," the court stated:

All citizens in so far as they hold views different from
the majority of their fellows are subject to such incon-
veniences. And this is especially true of those who hold
religious or moral beliefs which are looked upon with
disdain by the majority.   It is precisely every citizen's
right to be a "speckled bird" that our constitutions, state
and federal, seek to insure.   And solace for the embarrassment that is attendant upon holding such beliefs
must be found by the individual citizen in his own moral

---

[12] Mitchell v. McCall, 273 Ala 604, 143 S(2d) 629 (1962).

courage and strength of conviction, and not in a court of law.

The Supreme Court of Alabama thereby affirmed the judgment of the lower court saying that the girl did not have to wear the prescribed clothes, did not have to participate in all exercises, but did have to take physical education in the regular class to which she had been assigned.

§ 4.3 Authority of school officials to prohibit certain types of dress

Although one would find little in the school codes of the various states that would imply the grant of specific authority to school officers, administrators, and teachers to control the attire and personal appearance of pupils who attend the public school, few people would argue that school authorities may not prohibit any dress which could be proved to have an adverse effect upon the discipline and general well-being of the school. Unconventional dress or change in physical appearance which has been labeled as disturbing and distracting by school authorities has resulted often in the suspension of the pupil involved until the appropriate steps have been taken to rectify the situation. Reports of such action by administrators are found in the headlines of local and nationwide newspapers; however, through the cooperative efforts of school personnel, parents, and pupils throughout the country, incidents which have the potential for developing into unpleasant experiences have been avoided. When the action of school personnel has seemed to be in excess of their authority, unreasonable, or arbitrary and not resolved to the satisfaction of the school patrons affected, threats of litigation have followed the punitive measures taken. The threats for one reason or another have remained in most instances as threats; in a few instances the threats were substantiated by litigation.

After becoming familiar with the details of the early cases which the courts were asked to adjudicate, one can see the effect that changing customs may have upon the controls placed on pupil dress; but familiarization with and consideration of these cases will show the extent to which the courts will go to uphold decisions, rules, and regulations of school authorities when they have been made in good faith. In the first quarter of the twentieth century a school board adopted a resolution which stated, "The wearing of transparent hosiery, low-necked dress or any style of clothing tending toward immodesty in dress, or the use of face paint or cosmetics, is prohibited."[13] A pupil who had been asked to remove her make-up and not wear it to school again returned to school after being so instructed with talcum powder on her face. Denied admission to school for failure to obey the rule, Pearl Pugsley, eighteen years old, requested that a writ of mandamus be issued requiring her reinstatement.

The Supreme Court of Arkansas indicated that unless it could be shown that there was a clear abuse of discretion by the school board in adopting such a rule and that the rule was unreasonable, the court must uphold the rule regardless of whether the action of the school directors was considered wise by the court. Justice Smith expressed the opinion of the court:

Courts have other and more important functions to perform than that of hearing the complaints of disaffected pupils of the public schools against the rules and regulations promulgated by the school boards for the government of the schools. The courts have the right of review, for the reasonableness of such a rule is a judicial question, and the courts will not refuse to perform their functions in determining the reasonableness of such rules, when the question is presented. But, in doing so, it will be kept in mind that the directors are elected by the patrons of the schools over which they preside, and the election occurs annually. The directors are in close and intimate touch with the affairs of their respective districts, and know the conditions with which they have to deal. It will be remembered also that respect for constituted authority and obedience thereto is an essential lesson to qualify one for the duties of

---

[13] Pugsley v. Sellmeyer, 158 Ark 247, 250 SW 538 (1923).

citizenship, and that the schoolroom is an appropriate place to teach that lesson; so that the courts hesitate to substitute their will and judgment for that of the school boards which are delegated by law as the agencies to prescribe rules for the government of the public schools of the state, which are supported at the public expense.

The Supreme Court of Arkansas further ruled that since local conditions might exist which would justify the adoption of a rule of this nature to aid in the discipline of the school and since it was unnecessary to seek a reason for the adoption of such rule in order to uphold it, the court would not annul it.

The Supreme Court of North Dakota in *Stromberg* v. *French* ruled that a board of education may forbid pupils to wear metal heel plates when they caused more than normal damage to the floors and when noise and confusion was such as to affect the conduct and discipline of the school.[14]   At the beginning of the 1930-31 school year, the principal and superintendent noticed that not only were the hardwood floors of the halls and classrooms being damaged by boys wearing metal heel plates but that an undue disturbance was being created by noise of the heel plates.   Murray Stromberg was one of the boys who complied with the requests of the principal and superintendent to stop using the metal taps and, thus, avoid damage and disturbance in the school.   When his mother discovered that he had removed his heel plates, she instructed Murray to replace them.   Upon his return to school Murray was told that he would be refused admission until the taps were removed as requested.

The parents of the boy insisted that it was their prerogative to decide what apparel their child would wear to school and that the school in forbidding the wearing of heel plates was being arbitrary and unreasonable.   Stromberg attempted, through court action, to enjoin the school board from enforcing the rule which had been adopted on September 25.

_____

14 Stromberg v. French, 60 ND 750, 236 NW 477 (1931).

The record of the court showed that the school board had promulgated the rule to protect the school property for which they held a statutory responsibility and to maintain good order and discipline. The court explained that this was one of those instances in which the paramount right of the parent must give way to the interests of the public generally and that ". . . there was no hardship or indignity imposed upon the plaintiff or his son by it." In answer to the plaintiff's argument that if this rule were permitted to stand, others might be enacted which would result in giving a school board absolute authority to prescribe wearing apparel for children who wished to enjoy the privileges of public education, the court declared that the "safeguard of reasonableness" would always be considered.

Although Murray Stromberg was an excellent student of good conduct, the court concurred:

> Whatever he did was done without malice or willful disregard of rules and only because of parental command. It seems to us that even so his conduct amounted to insubordination. Any other construction put upon the term as used in the statute might result in an intolerable situation. No rule or regulation could be enforced, provided the parent directed the pupil not to observe it. So we hold that the action of Murray, though taken at the command of his parents, constituted insubordination within the meaning of that term as used in the statute.

In 1934 the school committee of Haverhill, Massachusetts, attempted to regulate membership in secret societies by enacting a prohibitory rule which included the statement that "the wearing of jerseys, sweaters, caps and other conspicuous evidence of membership in an unapproved secret organization is hereby forbidden on the school premises."[15] The petitioners sought to enjoin the school committee from enforcing the rule designed to abolish secret societies, but the Supreme Judicial Court of Massachusetts dismissed the petition saying that the expulsion of pupils violating

---

[15] Antell v. Stokes, 287 Mass 103, 191 NE 407 (1934).

the rule did not exceed the power conferred upon the committee by the legislature.

When the principal of a high school in Georgia refused to permit a female pupil to continue her attendance in classes while wearing slacks, the father petitioned the courts for a writ of mandamus directed at the principal.[16] J. L. Matheson, the plaintiff and father of the girl, maintained that the principal's act interfered with his rights guaranteed under certain provisions of the constitutions of the United States and Georgia. The Supreme Court of Georgia affirmed the judgment of the lower court which denied the writ on the technical grounds that the petition did not show the principal to be a public officer or the school to be a part of the state school system. Whether his unsuccessful attempts to gain a writ were a source of discouragement, whether the question became moot, or whether the plaintiff was able to resolve his grievance without further court action is not known; but no report is found to indicate that Matheson pursued the subject any further.

§ 4.4 Summary

Perusal of almost any daily newspaper for a period of a month or less usually will furnish one with sufficient evidence to conclude that schoolmen are concerned with, and in many instances, attempting to do something about the dress and personal appearance of the pupils in their charge. School personnel in various sections of the country are confronted almost daily by problems arising from the personal appearance of pupils. Through cooperative planning some of the schools are meeting with success in their attempts to improve the personal appearance of the student body. Whether the action which is taken by educators springs from the belief that improper dress has an ill effect upon the discipline of the school or that responsibility for developing habits of good grooming resides with the school, they may find difficulty in justifying their action unless due emphasis is placed upon the customs of the community, the purposes of the school, the needs of young

---

16 Matheson v. Brady, 202 Ga 500, 43 SE(2d) 703 (1947).

people, the influence of the action upon the future discipline and well-being of the school, and the legal obligations and limitations imposed upon the school. If all or any of these considerations is omitted from the planning of a program for improving dress, the school may be placed in a position which will render it less effective in serving the community of which it is a part.

All litigation concerning the dress of pupils has been confined to the twentieth century. One who has studied the subject would not expect to find statutes either specific or implied dealing with the authority of school officials to regulate the wearing apparel of pupils, but he would find that unconventional attire has been dealt with in ways limited only by the imagination of local school personnel. Perhaps because parents approve of the action taken by school authorities, because they feel that the control of dress is within the authority delegated to school officials, or because it is simpler to comply than litigate, only a few instances of court action have been reported when parents felt that the control exerted by the school was an invasion of parental rights. The power to take action under the general authority delegated by the legislature and the reasonableness of the action taken by school authorities have been the foci for rendering decisions concerning the differences presented to the courts. The cases which the courts have been called upon to review have dealt with the prescribing of uniforms for pupils in attendance, prescribing of attire for a particular activity of the school, and prohibiting apparel which was considered damaging to school property, morale, or discipline.

Few, if any, public schools today have regulations which require pupils in attendance to wear uniforms; but during the first quarter of this century, the practice was prevalent enough to produce three court cases brought by parents wishing to enjoin the enforcement of such a regulation. When a parent in Bainbridge, Georgia, sought to restrain the superintendent and trustees of the public schools from enforcing a rule which required male pupils of a certain age and height to wear a uniform, the Supreme Court of

Georgia, *McCaskill* v. *Bower, supra,* n 5, dismissed the petition which had been filed in opposition to the rule. The court's judgment was based on the grounds that the plaintiff had chosen the improper legal remedy to restrain enforcement of a school rule and had not alleged that the rule had been applied to his two sons.

Fifteen years later in *Jones* v. *Day, supra,* n 7, a father instituted proceedings on behalf of his son against the superintendent and trustees of a high school which required high school boys to wear khaki uniforms. The Supreme Court of Mississippi declared the rule valid as applied to boarding pupils, but the stipulation was made that the rule could be enforced only when pupils were under the care and custody of the school.

In 1928 a divided court dismissed the action brought by Julian Lamme, *Colorado ex rel. Lamme* v. *Buckland, supra,* n 11, against the school committee that had expelled his daughter from a public school for her refusal to comply with the rules and regulations which specified that uniforms were to be worn by girls. The Supreme Court of Colorado in quashing the writ ruled that the plaintiff had not exhausted the statutory remedy for grievances addressed against school rules before bringing his complaint to court.

The Supreme Court of Iowa in *Valentine* v. *Independent School District of Casey, supra,* n 8 declared unreasonable a rule which provided for withholding a diploma for refusal to wear a cap and gown in the graduation exercises. The court ruled that it was within the power of the local authorities to refuse participation in the ceremony to those who would not wear a cap and gown, but the court said that the granting of a diploma to a pupil who had fulfilled all requirements for graduation and who otherwise qualified for graduation was mandatory.

In 1912 the Supreme Court of Oklahoma in *Connell* v. *Gray, supra,* n 6, modified a lower court order in favor of Ruth Gray, who had been denied admission to Oklahoma Agricultural and Mechanical College for non-payment of fees which included a deposit for clothing and equipment to be used in the gymnasium. The court stated that although a fee might be charged for a uniform when funds were not appropriated, a pupil who supplied himself with such a uniform would not be subject to the fee.

Fifty years later the Supreme Court of Alabama, *Mitchell* v. *McCall, supra*, n 12, upheld the action of a school board which suspended a pupil who refused to participate in physical education because of her objection to the clothing worn. When school officials conceded that Eulene Mitchell would not be required to wear the costume that she and her parents considered "immodest and sinful" or to take part in exercises which they felt were immodest in the costume which she chose, the Mitchells expressed an additional objection to the girl's being placed in a class where others wore the prescribed dress. The court ruled that the pupil did not have to wear the prescribed dress and did not have to take part in exercises which offended her modesty, but the court upheld the school board in its refusal to provide a special class for the pupil who stood out like a "speckled bird" in the regular class.

In *Pugsley* v. *Sellmeyer, supra*, n 13, the court rendered a decision which said that a school board rule which prohibited the wearing of transparent hosiery, make-up, and low-necked dresses was within the discretionary power of the school board. Declaring the rule reasonable, the Arkansas court refused to annul the rule and emphasized that local school directors were closer to the situation and, therefore, in a better position than the courts to determine the necessity of such a rule.

The Supreme Court of North Dakota in *Stromberg* v. *French, supra*, n 14, pointed out that in most instances the right of parents was paramount but that public interest took precedent in this case over the prerogative of the parents. The court declared that a board of education was within its authority when it forbade pupils to wear metal heel plates which caused more than normal damage to the floors and when noise and confusion were such as to impair the good conduct and discipline of the school.

A prohibitory rule which was aimed at abolishing secret societies and which contained a statement forbidding the wearing of emblems or clothing indicative of membership in a secret society on the school premises was upheld in *Antell* v. *Stokes, supra,* n 15, by a Massachusetts court. The Supreme Judicial Court of Massachusetts dismissed the petition to enjoin the school committee from enforcing the antifraternity rule saying that the expulsion of pupils violating the rule did not exceed the authority conferred upon the committee by the legislature.

When a pupil was not permitted to continue attendance in her classes while wearing slacks, the father in *Matheson* v. *Brady, supra,* n 16, petitioned the court for a writ of mandamus to compel the principal to reinstate his daughter. The writ was denied on the technical grounds that the principal was not shown in the petition to be a public officer or the school to be a part of the state school system. No further steps were taken to amend the original petition.

Of the instances of litigation relating to the action taken by schoolmen in attempting to regulate the personal appearance of pupils, three petitions were dismissed solely on technical grounds. An examination of the remaining cases would indicate that local circumstances and customs as well as the degree of control exerted by the school played an important part in the final determination made by the courts. Unless local school boards can justify the enactment of rules and regulations by showing the adverse effects of clothing and personal appearance upon the welfare of the school, it is doubtful that local authorities will find court sanction for their action.

Chapter 5

AUTHORITY OF SCHOOL OFFICIALS TO ADOPT RULES AND REGULATIONS PERTAINING TO HEALTH

Through the years the parent usually has been considered responsible for the health and welfare of his children; but as daily contacts between individuals have become more numerous and interdependence has begun to hold more significance than in earlier days, others have come to recognize that the community welfare is dependent upon the well-being of its individual members. When one out of three young men in his late teens or early twenties was unable to meet the minimum physical qualifications when called for duty in the armed forces during World War II, the informed public became alarmed; and under this stimulus many people began to expound upon the necessity for better health care.[1] Since Theodore Roosevelt sent personally handwritten invitations to two hundred delegates to attend the first White House Conference On Children and Youth, government officials have continued to hold such conferences periodically; and each decade has witnessed an increased amount of time in the meetings being devoted to the discussion of health.[2] Professional literature, both educational and medical, is placing emphasis upon the type of health services which should be rendered by public agencies to individuals and groups. Although there is almost universal agreement that efforts should be made to maintain

---

[1] Werner Bloch, "Some Remarks On School Health Examinations," The Journal of School Health, XXX (November, 1960), p. 342.
[2] Richard Means, "Contributions of the White House Conferences On Children and Youth to School Health Education," The Journal of School Health, XXX (November, 1960), p. 324.

and protect good health and that poor health should be improved, there is not universal agreement as to how such a state should be accomplished.

§ 5.1 A broadened concept of school health services

Almost axiomatic to those in the teaching profession are the ideas that health is vital to learning and that the poor health of one pupil may not only be a contributory factor in the personal lack of accomplishment by the pupil but that it may also impede the progress of other members of the same class. Recognizing the importance of the psychological, emotional, and physical well-being to a person's optimum achievement and encouraged by the public interest in good health, schools throughout the United States have conducted investigations to discover the place of the school in relation to health services. These investigations in many instances have led schoolmen to assume or be assigned responsibilities formerly neglected or delegated to other agencies.

While some states have specific statutory provisions which designate the areas in which public agencies may operate, other state codes are general in nature in the delegation of responsibility for various health activities. The school by virtue of the number of people involved provides opportunities for the promotion of health and the prevention of disease. Since the health of children and the health of the community are so interrelated, health departments and school boards in some areas are combining or coordinating their efforts to furnish health programs to their vicinity. Today, the services offered by the school independently or cooperatively, either by statutory authorization, statutory implication, or by local initiative, vary from elaborate programs in school health, which include curriculum offerings and staffs professionally trained for health service, to daily health examinations, which the adults of today will recall from childhood as being a hand and fingernail inspection by the classroom teacher. The intent of many educators seems not only to prevent outbreaks of various diseases and future trouble which may endanger the physical health of pupils but to improve present performance by taking into consideration physical, emotional, and mental handicaps and making provisions for them.

Few schools have ventured into the treatment of illnesses; but since the latter part of the nineteenth century and the first part of the twentieth century, when health programs consisted almost exclusively of sanitation of the school and control of communicable diseases through immunization or isolation, the concept of school health services has broadened. The scope of school health programs may be found to encompass plans for health appraisal, for prevention and control of diseases, for identification of physical or mental deficiencies or strengths, for provisions for the physically or mentally exceptional child, for consultation with parents concerning health appraisal and possible corrective measures, and for administration of emergency care. Depending upon permissive legislation, statutory edict, or discretionary authority for the position that they take, school systems have set certain health prerequisites for enrollment and attendance in the public schools. Going one step further, some schools encourage or require the participation of pupils in health programs designed to detect or prevent diseases peculiar to their particular community. Parents by and large welcome or at least accept the health rules and regulations of their child's school, but occasionally objections are voiced to some particular aspect of the program. If school officials are to minimize the number of threats, challenges, and criticisms related to the health services of the school, they must consider the legal, ethical, and public relations aspects of the health rules and regulations which they are planning to adopt.

An investigation of the practices of various school districts would more than likely reveal many differences in the administration of school health services, but one could be justified in expecting to find that every school system does conduct some program related to the health of its pupils. An acquaintance with the programs conducted by the schools would serve to enlighten one as to the potential areas for court action by dissatisfied patrons. As many people urge early identification of health defects, both mental and physical, for the maximum welfare of the child, schoolmen are brought into a position of where the early identification in itself may stimulate court action. If one examines the judgment of the courts in the cases thus far adjudicated, he is in a better position to understand the responsibilities, obligations, and limitations of the public school in administering health programs.

§ 5.2 Requiring vaccination as a condition of school attendance

If the number of cases alone could be taken as any indication of the concern of parents over the controls exerted upon their child by school authorities, litigation resulting from objections to rules and regulations of school boards making vaccination a requirement for school attendance would indicate that the vaccination requirement would be among those areas of pupil control to hold a position of utmost concern. As one reviews the cases related to vaccination that have been considered by the courts in this country, he must keep in mind that each case was judged on the issues involved in that particular case and that as the first cases reached the courts, there was some controversy as to the benefits of vaccination as well as to the possible ill effects of it. Frequently, the plaintiffs contended that they opposed the rules and regulations requiring vaccinations upon the grounds that enforcement would endanger the health of the individual vaccinated, that the requirement was unreasonable and not within the power of the school board to make, and that vaccination was in opposition to certain religious convictions.

As long ago as the first cases were heard and as numerous as the cases may be, it is evident from the frequency and recency of litigation presented in this chapter that all issues concerning vaccination requirements have not yet been settled. In the presentation of reported cases concerning the authority of school boards to make vaccination a condition for school attendance, the cases will be categorized under three headings: authorization by statute; authorization by boards of health; authorization through discretionary power.

(a) *Authorization by statute.* When James Abeel was refused admission to the public schools of Santa Cruz because he had not complied with the vaccination act of California, the Supreme Court of California in 1890 rendered a decision, *Abeel* v. *Clark,* which was to lend guidance to other jurisdictions for years to come.[3] The court ruled that the legislature had the power to enact legislation ". . . to secure and maintain the health and prosperity of the state . . ." as long as the enactments were not unconstitutional. Justification for the legislation was seen in the attempt to protect pupils and the community from smallpox through vaccination, the ". . . best method known to medical science to lessen the liability to infection with the disease."

Since the decision in *Abeel* v. *Clark,* courts, without exception, have upheld school boards in enforcing the legislative acts concerning vaccination; and when the acts of the legislature have been attacked as being unconstitutional, the courts have ruled that the legislation was a proper exercise of police power of the state and not in violation of constitutional rights.[4] In explanation of the police power of the state, the Supreme Court of California said:

---

[3] Abeel v. Clark, 84 Cal 226, 24 Pac 383 (1890).

[4] Bissell v. Davison, 65 Conn 183, 32 Atl 348 (1894); In re Walters, 32 NYS 322 (1895); Field v. Robinson, 198 Pa 638, 48 Atl 873 (1901); French v. Davidson, 143 Cal 658, 77 Pac 663 (1904); Viemeister v. White, 179 NY 235, 72 NE 97 (1904); Stull v. Reber, 215 Pa 156, 64 Atl 419 (1906); State ex rel. Milhoof v. Board of Education of Barberton, 76 OhioSt 297, 81 NE 568 (1907); State ex rel. McFadden v. Shorrock, 55 Wash 208, 104 Pac 214 (1909); Lee v. Marsh, 230 Pa 351, 79 Atl 564 (1911); Spofford v. Carlton, 238 Mass 528, 131 NE 314 (1921); Barber v. School Board of Rochester, 82 NH 426, 135 Atl 159 (1926); Cram v. School Board of Manchester, 82 NH 495, 136 Atl 263 (1927); Mosier v. Barren County Board of Health, 308 Ky. 829, 215 SW(2d) 967 (1948); Sadlock v. Board of Education of Carlstadt, 137 NJL 85, 58 A(2d) 218 (1948); Dunham v. Board of Education of City School Dist. of Cincinnati, 98 NE(2d) 594 (Ohio, 1950); State ex rel. Dunham v. Board of Education of City School Dist. of Cincinnati, 154 OhioSt 469, 96 NE(2d) 413 (1951); Ohio ex rel. Dunham v. Board of Education of the City School Dist. of Cincinnati, 341 US 915, 95 LEd ——, 71 SCt 736 (1951); Anderson v. State, 84 GaApp 259, 65 SE(2d) 848 (1951); Board of Education of Mountain Lakes v. Maas, 56 NJSuper 245, 152 A(2d) 394 (1959).

Police regulations generally interfere with the liberty of the citizen in one sense. To arrest a man for a breach of peace is an interference with his liberty. It is no valid objection to a police regulation that it prevents a person from doing something that he wants to do, or that he might do if it were not for the regulation. When we have determined that the act is within the police power of the state, nothing further need be said. The rest is to be left to the discretion of the lawmaking power. It is for that power to say whether vaccination shall be had as to all school children who have not been vaccinated all the time, or whether it shall be resorted to only when smallpox is more ordinarily prevalent and dangerous.[5]

When his ten-year old son was excluded from school in accordance with the provisions of the act requiring vaccination of those who attend the public schools of New York, the plaintiff in *Viemeister* v. *White* pointed out that no special danger from smallpox existed in the community.[6] Justice Vann replied that the state was within its power in trying to prevent the spread of contagious diseases and that although some maintained that vaccination was not a preventive of smallpox, this reason in itself was not sufficient to declare the act void:

> While we do not decide and cannot decide what vaccination is a preventive of smallpox, we take judicial notice of the fact that this is the common belief of the people of the state, and with this fact as a foundation we hold that the statute in question is a health law, enacted in reasonable and proper exercise of the police power. It operates impartially upon all children in the public schools, and is designed, not only for their protection, but for the protection of all the people of the state. The relator's son is excluded from school only until he complies with the law to protect the health of all, himself and his family included. No right conferred or secured by the Constitution was violated by that law, or by the action of the school authorities based thereon.

---

5 French v. Davidson, 143 Cal 658, 77 Pac 663 (1904).
6 Viemeister v. White, 179 NY 235, 72 NE 97 (1904).

The Supreme Court of New Hampshire overruled the exception of the plaintiff in *Cram* v. *School Board of Manchester* that he would not permit his child to be vaccinated because ". . . vaccination consist of performing a surgical operation by injecting a poison, the ingredients of which are not known, into the blood of said daughter and that will endanger her health and life. . . ."[7] The court ruled that the vaccination act did not deny him of his liberty, health, and happiness as guaranteed by the constitutions of New Hampshire and the United States. A similar decision was rendered in *Mosier* v. *Barren County Board of Health* when two chiropractors expressed their beliefs as being opposed to vaccination.[8] The Kentucky court said that if a child was physically able to attend school, he was able to be vaccinated; that religious beliefs did not permit one to endanger the health of a community; and that the requirement was not in violation of the United States Constitution.

In upholding school boards in their attempts to enforce legislative enactments concerning vaccination for smallpox, the court has ruled that it is not necessary for a school board to provide a free education for a child who was refused admission to the public schools for failure to show evidence of immunization against smallpox.[9] A school board may continue to enforce legislation requiring vaccination although the vicinity has not been affected by smallpox for forty years; the court indicated that the absence of smallpox for forty years did not insure continued safety from the disease.[10] Not only have courts ruled that children may be excluded from school for not complying with the statute making vaccination a condition for school attendance, but it is within the power of the legislature to prescribe how the immunization is to be administered.[11] When a

---

[7] Cram v. School Board of Manchester, 82 NH 495, 136 Atl 263 (1927).

[8] Mosier v. Barren County Board of Health, 308 Ky 829, 215 SW(2d) 967 (1948).

[9] State ex rel. Dunham v. Board of Education of City School Dist. of Cincinnati, 154 OhioSt 469, 96 NE(2d) 413 (1951).

[10] Stull v. Reber, 215 Pa 156, 64 Atl 419 (1906).

[11] Lee v. Marsh, 230 Pa 351, 79 Atl 564 (1911).

child presents a certificate as provided by statute that he is physically unable to be vaccinated, the certificate does not provide permanent exemption, and the school may require presentation of another certificate at some later date.[12]

A case that grew out of permissive legislation giving boards of education the authority to adopt rules to require vaccination for smallpox and immunization for diphtheria was *Board of Education of Mountain Lakes* v. *Maas*.[13] The defendant, a Christian Scientist, refused to have the Greek children who were visiting in her home for a twelve-month period vaccinated against smallpox and immunized against diphtheria, claiming that the school board rule interfered with her constitutional rights of religious freedom. When she continued to bring the children to school after their suspension, the school board brought action aimed at enforcing its regulation. Judge Goldman, delivering the opinion of the court, stated:

> Defendant is neither the parent nor legal guardian of the three children whom she brought from Greece . . . At the time she sought their admittance to the Mountain Lakes public schools she occupied a position no stronger than that of foster mother *pro tem* — for the period of one year during which the immigration authorities permitted the children to be with her. It is stipulated that the children did not come of Christian Science parents; . . . it would appear they had been brought up in the Greek Orthodox Church. They were vaccinated before coming to this country, and this apparently without objection on religious grounds. The objection now made to immunization is solely defendant's. . . .
>
> Insofar as defendant seeks to assert her own right to religious freedom, she has no standing. The vaccination and immunization requirement does not apply to her. She has no personal responsibility for the children's re-

---

[12] Spofford v. Carlton, 238 Mass 528, 131 NE 314 (1921); Barber v. School Board of Rochester, 82 NH 426, 135 Atl 159 (1926).

[13] Board of Education of Mountain Lakes v. Maas, 56 NJSuper 245, 152 A(2d) 394 (1959).

ligious upbringing other than in the religion in which
they were raised.

The court further declared that the actions of the school
board were neither arbitrary nor capricious since a uniform
policy had been established, maintained, and applied to
all alike since 1953.

Reviewing the reports from the action in various jurisdictions pertaining to vaccination statutes, one will encounter
in most cases since 1904, reference to the decision of the
United States Supreme Court in *Jacobson* v. *Massachusetts*.[14] Justice Harlan delivered the opinion of the court
concerning the validity of a Massachusetts act which gave
local boards of health the power to require and enforce
vaccination except upon children unfit for vaccination if
in its opinion it deemed such action necessary to the
preservation of public health and safety. Declaring that
smallpox had been prevalent, the city of Cambridge adopted
a resolution that required all inhabitants of the city to be
vaccinated. Jacobson, stating that the regulation denied
him rights secured through the Fourteenth Amendment
of the United States Constitution refused to be vaccinated;
and action was taken against him.

Upholding the statute, Justice Harlan stated:

We come, then, to inquire whether any right given or
secured by the Constitution is invaded by the statute as
interpreted by the state court. The defendant insists
that his liberty is invaded when the state subjects him
to fine or imprisonment for neglecting or refusing to submit to vaccination; that a compulsory vaccination law
is unreasonable; arbitrary, and oppressive, and, therefore, hostile to the inherent right of every freeman to
care for his own body and health in such a way as
to him seems best; and that the execution of such a law
against one who objects to vaccination, no matter for
what reason, is nothing short of an assault upon his
person. But the liberty secured by the Constitution of

---

[14] Jacobson v. Massachusetts, 197 US 11, 49 LEd 643, 25 SCt 358
(1904).

the United States to every person within its jurisdiction does not impart an absolute right in each person to be, at all times and in all circumstances, wholly freed from restraint. There are manifold restraints to which every person is necessarily subject for the common good. On any other basis organized society could not exist with safety to its members.

The United States Supreme Court further reasoned:

Society based on the rule that each one is a law unto himself would soon be confronted with disorder and anarchy. Real liberty for all could not exist under the operation of a principle which recognizes the right of each individual person to use his own, whether in respect of his person of his property, regardless of the injury that may be done to others. This court has more than once recognized it as a fundamental principle that "persons and property are subjected to all kinds of restraints and burdens in order to secure the general comfort, health, and prosperity of the state; of the perfect right of the legislature to do which no question ever was, or upon acknowledged general principles ever can be, made, so far as natural persons are concerned.

Not only have the courts ruled that school boards are within their authority to support and enforce vaccination requirements set forth in statutes, but courts also have ruled that boards of education must refuse to admit to the public school any child who has not been vaccinated when the statute so requires.[15] When a school board in California refused to enforce the act requiring vaccination for public school attendance, the court stated:

The statute is not directory, but mandatory. . . . It is the plain duty of the trustees, and they are directed by the express terms of the statute, to exclude from the public

---

[15] Pennsylvania ex rel. Carson v. Rowe, 218 Pa 168, 67 Atl 56 (1907); State Board of Health v. Board of Trustees of Watsonville School Dist., 13 CalApp 514, 110 Pac 137 (1910); Pennsylvania v. Wilkins, 75 PaSuper 305 (1920); Pennsylvania ex rel. Schaffer v. Wilkins, 271 Pa 523, 115 Atl 887 (1922).

schools any child or person who has not been vaccinated.
. . . If the trustees could use their discretion, and of
their own will at times exclude and at other times admit
to the schools children who have not been vaccinated,
or if the trustees could exclude some children and admit
others, the law would be uncertain and of little value.
. . . The duty devolves upon defendants by virtue of
their office to exclude such children. They must obey
and not question the law. . . . While in office it is their
duty . . . to see that the law is enforced, and this
whether the law is popular or unpopular, or whether they
believe in the vaccination of children or otherwise.[16]

When a state has a compulsory school attendance law
and a law directing or permitting boards of education to
require vaccination as a condition of school attendance,
there is disagreement in the courts as to whether a parent
whose child has been excluded from school for noncompliance with the vaccination requirement can be found
in violation of the compulsory attendance law. Some courts
take the position that the child has been excluded through
an act of the school board and that the parent is not guilty
of keeping the child from school in the meaning of the
compulsory attendance statute.[17] An Ohio court explained:

The compulsory education act was obviously intended
to meet the cases where the parent was indifferent to the
attendance of the child and made no effort to cause
the child to attend the schools. The act was certainly
not intended to be used as a means of enforcing any rule
which the board of education in the plentitude of its
general power sees fit to adopt.

✳   ✳   ✳

If exclusion from failure to comply with the rule of a
public school as to vaccination is no defense to a prosecu-

16 State Board of Health v. Board of Trustees of Watsonville School
Dist., supra n. 15.

17 Pennsylvania v. Smith, 9 PaDist 625 (1900); Ohio v. Turney, 31
Ohio CC 222 (1909); Shappee v. Curtis, 127 NYS 33 (1911); Ohio v.
Dunham, 154 OhioSt 63, 93 NE(2d) 286 (1950).

tion under the compulsory education act, then the exclusion for violation of a similar rule as to private or parochial or other districts schools would be no defense and we would then be face to face with a compulsory vaccination law.[18]

The plaintiff in *Marsh* v. *Earle* complained that the Pennsylvania courts had placed an unconstitutional interpretation on the compulsory attendance and vaccination laws of that state.[19] The Pennsylvania court dismissed the petition of Marsh for the lack of jurisdiction, because the laws complained of were within the police power of the state and constitutional, and because the plaintiff had not exhausted the remedies open to him before resorting to the courts. Other courts have taken the position that a pupil excluded from school for nonvaccination is subject to the compulsory school attendance law and that although a parent sends or brings his unvaccinated child to school after exclusion, he is still subject to the penalties of violating the attendance law if the school does not admit the child.[20] The Court of Appeals of New York held:

If indifferent or selfish parents for ulterior purposes, such as the desire to place young children at labor instead of school, or from capricious or recalcitrant motives, may be allowed to manufacture easy excuses for not sending their children to school, a ready method will have been developed for evading the statute compelling such attendance, and, if the statute which requires parents to see to it that their children attend and take advantage of this school system may be lightly and easily evaded, the purposes of the state in providing and insisting on edu-

---

18 Ohio v. Turney, 31 OhioCC 222 (1909).
19 Marsh v. Earle, 24 FSupp 385 (1938).
20 People v. Ekerold, 211 NY 386, 105 NE 670 (1914); People v. McIlwain, 151 NYS 366 (1915); Commonwealth v. Aiken, 64 PaSuper 96 (1916); Commonwealth v. Butler, 76 PaSuper 113 (1920); Commonwealth v. Green, 286 Mass 585, 168 NE 101 (1929); State v. Drew, 89 NH 54, 192 Atl 629 (1937); Commonwealth v. Childs, 299 Mass 367, 12 NE(2d) 814 (1938); In re Marsh, 140 PaSuper 472, 14 A(2d) 368 (1940); In re Whitmore, 47 NYS(2d) 143 (1944); Anderson v. State, 84 Ga App 259, 65 SE(2d) 848 (1951).

cation will be frustrated and impaired. Failure to comply with the statute ought not to be excused except for some good reason.

❋   ❋   ❋

It is hardly to be assumed that when the Legislature passed the later statute there had slipped from its theoretical mind remembrance of the other law providing a very important condition of attendance at public schools, and, if it had purposed that a child might be excused from attendance by reason of unwillingness of its parent to have it vaccinated, I cannot but believe that something would have been said on the subject. . . .

If a parent may escape all obligation under the statute requiring him to send his children to school by simply alleging that he does not believe in vaccination, the policy of the state to give some education to all children, if necessary by compelling measures, will become more or less of a farce under existing legislation.[21]

Thirty years later a mother in New York who refused to have her child vaccinated because of her religious scruples was told by the court:

In a democracy laws are not made to meet the predilections of individuals, nor to feed mistaken views which an individual might hold, when that view is detrimental to the people as a whole. Laws are made for the protection of all, and such laws are enforced even if the law is hateful to some individual.

❋   ❋   ❋

I am not unmindful of the fact that under the Constitution of the United States of America, and under the Constitution of New York, particularly under the Bill of Rights, no law may be made to abridge or interfere with the right of any person in the worship of God as his conscience dictates, in particular the conscience of the person who worships God and the way in which God is worshipped by such person. The Founders of the Republic and the framers of the Constitution of the United States of

---

[21] People v. Ekerold, 211 NY 386, 105 NE 670 (1914).

America and the people approving same did not intend that the law would protect a person who might conceive of a God in a manner which might endanger the lives of the community in which such person might live.[22]

(b) Authorization by boards of health. In the absence of specific statutory enactments requiring pupils to be vaccinated, state departments of health and local agencies motivated by their responsibility for the welfare of the public have deemed it wise and necessary to enact resolutions which prohibit school attendance for those not vaccinated and have called upon boards of education to enforce their orders. The courts have not consistently held such enactments to be within the power of the health department; however, little difference of opinion may be found among the courts when an epidemic of smallpox was present or there existed a threat of immediate danger to the residents of a community. Without exception, when emergency measures were prescribed, the courts have upheld the boards of health in their attempts to protect the health of a community through an immunization program.[23]

During a threat of an epidemic of smallpox, the board of health in Terre Haute, Indiana, notified the local school board of its order excluding unvaccinated persons from the public schools to prevent the introduction and spread of the disease.[24] When the school board, acting upon the order of the board of health, excluded a child from school, the father brought action against the superintendent and

---

[22] In re Whitmore, 47 NYS(2d) 143 (1944).

[23] Blue v. Beach, 155 Ind 121, 56 NE 89 (1900); State ex rel. Cox v. Board of Education of Salt Lake City, 21 Utah 401, 60 Pac 1013 (1900); State ex rel. Horne v. Beil, 157 Ind 25, 60 NE 672 (1901); State ex rel. Freeman v. Zimmerman, 86 Minn 353, 90 NW 783 (1902); Board of Trustees of Highland Park Graded Common School Dist. No. 46 v. McMurtry, 169 Ky 457, 184 SW 390 (1916); Bright v. Beard, 132 Minn 375, 157 NW 501 (1916); Hagler v. Larner, 284 Ill 547, 120 NE 575 (1918); State ex rel. Lehman v. Partlow, 119 Wash 316, 205 Pac 420 (1922); People ex rel. Hill v. Board of Education of Lansing, 224 Mich 388, 195 NW 95 (1923); Vonnegurt v. Baun, 206 Ind 172, 188 NE 677 (1934); Auten v. Board of Directors of Special School Dist. of Little Rock, 83 Ark 431, 104 SW 130 (1907).

[24] Blue v. Beach, 155 Ind 121, 56 NE 89 (1900).

teacher involved in the exclusion claiming that there was only one case of smallpox in the state and none in Terre Haute, that vaccination was dangerous and not a preventive of smallpox, that some children in "feeble health" were exempted from the order, and that rules of this nature could be made only by the legislature. The Supreme Court of Indiana noted that although there was no express statute in the state making vaccination a condition of attending school, the action of the school board and board of health could be justified only as a public emergency. The court emphasized that the board of health had seen such an emergency and that the superintendent of schools had directed that the child not be admitted on that basis. The court said:

> It is true, as insisted, that the privilege of children in this state to attend the public schools is guaranteed by the constitution . . . It is equally true, however, that they are frequently denied this privilege, by reason of their refusal to submit to the proper rules of school discipline. There is no express law in this state authorizing the expulsion from school of boisterous or disobedient pupils. That a rule to this effect upon the part of school officials or teachers may be enforced, no one will controvert. If expulsion can result from the violation of a rule, the object of which is to promote the morals of the scholars, and the efficiency of the school in general, certainly one which is intended and calculated to promote the health of the scholars ought to be sustained.

Other courts have ruled to the same effect: if an epidemic was present or reasonable apprehension of danger of smallpox existed, boards of health were within the exercise of their power to order the exclusion of unvaccinated children in order to secure the welfare of others.[25] A physician's

---

25 State ex rel. Cox v. Board of Education of Salt Lake City, 21 Utah 401, 60 Pac 1013 (1900); State ex rel. Freeman v. Zimmerman, 86 Minn 353, 90 NW 783 (1902); Hagler v. Larner, 284 Ill 547, 120 NE 575 (1918); State ex rel. Lehman v. Partlow, 119 Wash 316, 205 Pac 420 (1922); Vonnegurt v. Baun, 206 Ind 172, 188 NE 677 (1934).

certificate of vaccination may be required of a pupil by a school board under conditions requiring vaccination.[26] Courts have further indicated that school boards, whose operations are rarely placed under the jurisdiction and command of health departments, in an emergency must enforce the rules of health departments concerning vaccination even if they do not agree with the measure taken.[27]

Under the authority granted it by the state board of health, a county board of health adopted a rule that all children must present a certificate of vaccination to attend school and called upon the school officers to enforce the rule.[28] Evidence was presented showing the presence of smallpox in the neighboring area and the possible danger in the immediate area. Considering the refusal of the school trustees to enforce the regulation, the Indiana court said:

> Local boards of health are created and authorized by the legislature, and duty bound to adopt and enforce rules and regulations for the arrest and prevention of contagious and infectious diseases in their respective jurisdictions, whenever the necessity therefore arises. The question of necessity must, from the very nature of the object to be attained, rest within the discretion and judgment of the board of health which seeks to adopt and enforce the rule. . . . The appellees, as officers charged with the public duty of managing the schools of Bluffton, are the proper persons to be called upon to enforce the rule in question in such schools.

The board of trustees looked to the courts for support when it brought suit against the city board of health and the county health officer to enjoin them from enforcing an order requiring all children attending public schools

---

[26] Auten v. Board of Directors of Special School Dist. of Little Rock, 83 Ark 431, 104 SW 130 (1907).

[27] State ex rel. Horne v. Biel, 157 Ind 25, 60 NE 672 (1901); **Board of Trustees of Highland Park Graded Common School Dist. No. 46 v. McMurtry, 169 Ky 457, 184 SW 390 (1916);People ex rel. Hill v. Board of Education of Lansing, 224 Mich 388, 195 NW 95 (1923).**

[28] State ex rel. Horne v. Biel, 157 Ind 25, 60 NE 672 (1901).

to be vaccinated if they had not been in the last seven years.[29] The Kentucky court upheld the board of health and the county health officer in cases where danger from smallpox existed by saying:

> In the very nature of things it would be utterly impracticable for the legislative department of the state to undertake to define the conditions that must exist before these boards could take such action as might be necessary to control situations that are constantly coming up in various forms; and so if these agencies of the state created for the purpose of conserving the health of the people are to accomplish the objects for which they are created, they must needs be given authority to take such prompt and effective action, in each case as it comes up, as in the exercise of their reasonable judgment and discretion may be deemed necessary to meet the exigencies of the occasion.

In granting a writ of mandamus to require a board of education to enforce a health regulation which excluded pupils who were not vaccinated from public school, the Supreme Court of Michigan said:

> We are plowing no virgin field in considering the questions here involved. Numerous decisions . . . have considered the questions now before us. They are not all in accord and in some instances are not reconcilable. There is, however, a very marked trend in them in one direction, that which upholds the right of the state, in the exercise of its police power and in the interest of the public health, to enact such laws, such rules and regulations, as will prevent the spread of this dread disease.
>
> *   *   *
>
> When we consider that one child may innocently communicate the disease to all its playmates in school, and realize how quickly the scourge spreads, unless restrained, it becomes evident that courts ought not to stay the hands

---

[29] Board of Trustees of Highland Park Graded Common School Dist. v. McMurtry, 169 Ky 457, 184 SW 390 (1916).

of an administrative body, seeking to protect the public
health, unless clearly convinced that the board is acting
arbitrarily and in abuse of discretion. Courts ought not
to under such circumstances with pencil and paper figure
out percentages and probabilities, and say to such board
we will substitute our judgment for yours, and, unless
a certain precentage of the population is stricken, you
may not act.[30]

Although courts have generally agreed that health departments are within their authority to prescribe regulations
concerning vaccination in emergencies, the courts are
divided in their opinions as to whether health departments
and agencies of the city may call upon school boards to
enforce their rules or regulations requiring vaccination for
school attendance when there is no immediate danger of
a smallpox epidemic. Some courts have ruled that in the
absence of an epidemic or threatened epidemic and without
specific statutory authority it is an unreasonable exercise
of power exerted by a board of health to legislate that
children may not attend public schools unless they have
been vaccinated.[31]   An Illinois court declared that a rule
requiring the temporary exclusion of an unvaccinated child
to prevent the spread of smallpox might be reasonable; but
the court pointed out that after danger had passed, the rule
could not be justified although it had been made under
the direction of the state board of health.[32]   The Supreme
Court of Illinois, two years later, upheld the decision of
the appellate court and added:

> . . . the right or privilege of attending the public schools
> is given by law to every child of proper age of the

---

[30] People ex rel. Hill v. Board of Education of Lansing, 224 Mich
388, 195 NW 95 (1923).
[31] School Directors v. Breen, 60 IllApp 201 (1895); Potts v. Breen, 167
Ill. 67, 47 NE 81 (1897); State ex rel. Adams v. Burdge, 95 Wis 390,
70 NW 347 (1897); People ex rel. La Baugh v. Board of Education of
Dist. No. 2, 177 Ill 572, 52 NE 850 (1899); Osborn v. Russell, 64 Kan
507, 68 Pac 60 (1902); People ex rel. Jenkins v. Board of Education
of Chicago, 234 Ill 422, 84 NE 1046 (1908); Rhea v. Board of Education of Devils Lake Special School Dist., 41 ND 449, 171 NW 103 (1919).
[32] School Directors v. Breen, 60 IllApp 201 (1895).

state, and there is nowhere to be found any provision of law prescribing vaccination as a condition precedent to the exercise of this right.

❖   ❖   ❖

The power to compel vaccination, or to require it as a condition precedent to the exercise of some right or privilege guaranteed to the citizen by public law, can be derived from no other source than the general police power of the state, and can be justified upon no other ground than as a necessary means of preserving the public health. Without the necessity, or reasonable grounds upon which to conclude that such necessity exists, the power does not exist. As such the board of health has no more power over the public schools than over private schools or other public assemblages, and its order applying to public schools only, requiring vaccination as a prerequisite to the exercise of the right to attend a public school could be justified only upon reasonable grounds appearing that the contagion of smallpox would more likely originate in or be disseminated from the public schools than from other assemblages.[33]

The courts have pointed out, without reluctance, that boards of health are administrative bodies not legislative.[34] Unless an emergency exists requiring action in the form of a vaccination rule, the exercise of duties by the health departments should be confined to administrative matters reasoned the courts.

Hill, a teacher, felt ". . . that he had no right or authority as teacher to reject any pupil that offered to attend . . ."and refused to prohibit admittance of unvaccinated children to school as ordered by the county health department.[35] Receiving support from the board of trustees, Hill sought injunctive action against the county health department which was attempting to enforce the order requiring

---

[33] Potts v. Breen, 167 Ill 67, 47 NE 81 (1897).
[34] State ex rel. Adams v. Burdge, 95 Wis 390, 70 NW 347 (1897); People ex rel. Jenkins v. Board of Education of Chicago, 234 Ill 422, 84 NE 1045 (1908).
[35] Hill v. Bickers, 171 Ky 703, 188 SW 766 (1916).

teachers and pupils to be vaccinated. The claim was made by Hill that there was no outbreak of smallpox, that communications with other communities were limited, and that residents of the community strongly objected to the vaccination rule. The Court of Appeals of Kentucky upheld and declared the order of the health department reasonable and necessary. The court told the teacher that unprofessional opinions might endanger the lives of all in the community and that "matters of such grave importance are not to be decided according to the whims of laymen."

Two cases which were considered and in which one opinion was delivered by the Supreme Court of Arkansas involved the validity of a requirement for vaccination by the state board of health although an epidemic did not threaten.[36] The court admitted that the state board of health was not given power to control schools, but the court further explained that the health board's attempts to control the spread of disease by preventing association with unvaccinated people did not constitute an infringement on teacher or pupil rights:

> It would not be contended that parents and guardians could send their children to school unclad and unfed. Other reasonable health regulations are just as important as food and clothing.
>
>   *   *   *
>
> The virtue of vaccination as a preventive of smallpox cannot be doubted. It is the generally known and accepted treatment for the prevention of this loathsome disease. We cannot say that under the prevailing conditions the adoption and promulgation of such a rule was either unreasonable or unnecessary.

The Supreme Court of Arkansas in *Allen* v. *Ingalls* stated that a school board did not abuse its discretion in adopting and enforcing a rule in accordance with a regulation of the board of health and that they were within their power when they refused to accept a pupil vaccinated by the

---

[36] State v. Martin, 134 Ark 420, 204 SW 622 (1918); Brazil v. State, 134 Ark 420, 204 SW 622 (1918).

homeopathic method.[37] Twenty years later the Arkansas court again ruled that a requirement of compulsory vaccination for public school attendance was not arbitrary, capricious, unreasonable, or in violation of rights guaranteed by the United States Constitution when Frank Seubold filed suit against a school board which had refused his children admittance to school on behalf of the state.[38]

When some schools, acting upon the terms of a city ordinance, refused to admit unvaccinated children to school, their action was challenged. Although no danger of an epidemic of smallpox was present, the courts in every instance upheld the school boards and declared the ordinances valid and promotion of health within the scope of the responsibilities of a city.[39] When the parent of a child sought to recover damages for the "unlawful" exclusion of his child and to have a city ordinance requiring vaccination declared void, a Texas court said:

> There is nothing known to the law broader than the long arm of police power to protect the inhabitants of a city in its health, and consequently against the ravages of disease. The power to eliminate disease of every kind that jeopardizes the health of her citizens and keeps a clean, sanitary, and healthy city is paramount to almost all other considerations.
>
>   ❖   ❖   ❖
>
> If, the city acting under its broad powers "to enforce vaccination," the test of such power be that it could be only enforced during time of epidemic, after many had been consigned to the grave for the want of it, it would indeed be a farce.[40]

----

[37] Allen v. Ingalls, 182 Ark 991, 33 SW(2d) 1099 (1931).

[38] Seubold v. Fort Smith Special School Dist., 218 Ark 560, 237 SW(2d) 884 (1951).

[39] Herbert v. Demopolis School Board of Education, 197 Ala 617, 73 So 321 (1916); New Braunfels v. Waldschmidt, 109 Tex 302, 207 SW 303 (1918); Zucht v. San Antonio School Board, 170 SW 840 (Texas, 1914); Zucht v. King, 225 SW 267 (Texas, 1920); Zucht v. King, 260 US 174, 43 SCt 24 (Texas, 1922); Hartman v. May, 168 Miss 477, 151 So 737 (1934).

[40] Zucht v. King, 225 SW 267 (Texas, 1920).

The court added in answer to the plaintiff's contention that some pupils were permitted to attend school without vaccination ". . . were not performing a public duty, but cannot affect the validity of the law." Upon appeal to the United States Supreme Court, Zucht petitioned that the ordinance in question violated the due process and equal protection clauses of the Fourteenth Amendment and was, therefore, unconstitutional.[41] The Supreme Court of the United States dismissed the writ of error by saying that it had been settled in *Jacobson* v. *Massachusetts,* 197 U.S. 11, 25 SupCt 358 ". . . that it is within the police power of a state to provide for compulsory vaccination."

(c) *Authorization through discretionary power.* An epidemic of smallpox in nearby cities, a case of smallpox in the city, and the request of the board of health prompted the board of education in Williamsport, Pennsylvania, to adopt a resolution making vaccination a requisite for school attendance. Duffield, whose child was excluded from school as a result of noncompliance with the resolution, sought a writ of mandamus to compel the school to admit his child.[42] Although the school board had not received authorization by specific statute to pass the health regulation in question, the court considered the resolution reasonable under the circumstances and emphasized the reluctance of courts to interfere with the discretionary power of school boards ". . . when that discretion is honestly and impartially exercised. . . ." A Missouri court made a similar disposition of a case in its refusal to declare a school board rule requiring vaccination unreasonable and said:

> In the nature of things, it must rest with the boards of education to determine what regulations are needful for a safe and proper management of the schools, and for the physical and moral health of the pupils entrusted to their care. If such regulations are not oppressive or arbitrary, the courts cannot, or should not, interfere.[43]

---

[41] Zucht v. King, 260 US 174, 43 SCt 24 (1922).

[42] Duffield v. School Dist. of Williamsport, 162 Pa 476, 29 Atl 742 (1894).

[43] In re Rebenack, 62 MoApp 8 (1895).

There was not a case of smallpox in a city when a father was granted a writ of mandamus to compel the city board of education to admit for instruction his child whom it had suspended for failure to comply with its resolution requiring vaccination. The child returned to school; but on the day of his return, the school board received notification from the state and county health boards that smallpox was prevalent in a nearby city. The child was suspended again, and the father brought action against the school board.[44] The court held that the board was not in contempt in that the child had been readmitted as ordered and that an emergency existed which justified suspension until the danger was removed.

The Supreme Court of Michigan, with two judges dissenting, ruled that a school board had exceeded its power in adopting a vaccination requirement in the absence of specific statutory authority and in the absence of an epidemic.[45] The spokesman for the majority pointed out that the children involved were in good health, that they had not been exposed to smallpox, that they were subject to the compulsory school law, and that "the effect of the rule adopted by the school board is to compel the vaccination of the child, or subject him and the parents to the penalties of the law."

The Michigan court further reasoned:

The board of education is a creature of the statute. It possesses only such powers as the statute gives it. The legislature has said who may and should attend the public schools. It has nowhere undertaken to confer the power upon the school board to change these conditions by passing a general, continuing rule excluding children from the public schools until they comply with conditions not imposed upon them by the legislative branch of the government. In what I have said I do not mean to intimate that during the prevalence of diphtheria or smallpox, or any other epidemic of contagious disease, in a school

---

44 Glover v. Board of Education of Lead, 14 SD 139, 84 NW 761 (1900).
45 Mathews v. Board of Education of School Dist. No. 1 of Kalamazoo, 127 Mich 530, 86 NW 1036 (1901).

district, the board may not, under its general powers, temporarily close the schools, or temporarily say who shall be excluded from the schools until the epidemic passed; but what I do say is that the legislature has not undertaken to give them the power, when no epidemic of contagious disease exists or is imminent in the district, to pass a general, continuing rule which would have the effect of a general law excluding all pupils who will not submit to vaccination.

Other courts presented with evidence that danger of smallpox was imminent have upheld vaccination rules adopted by school boards in the exercise of their discretionary power.[46] The city of Durham, North Carolina, had suffered a smallpox epidemic in the spring preceding the adoption of a school board rule requesting teachers and pupils to show evidence of vaccination before presenting themselves for attendance at school.[47] Although it was asserted by the plaintiff that his daughter would suffer ill effects from vaccination, the Supreme Court of North Carolina upheld the school board in the child's exclusion from school and stated:

> The fact that it would be dangerous to vaccinate the plaintiff's daughter, owing to her physical condition, would be a defense for her to an order for general compulsory vaccination . . . but is no reason why she should be excepted from a resolution excluding from school all children who have not been vaccinated. That she cannot safely be vaccinated may make it preferable that she herself should run the risk of taking the smallpox, but is no reason that the children of the public school should be exposed to like risk of infection, through her, or others in like case.

---

[46] Hutchins v. School Committee of Durham, 137 NC 68, 49 SE 46 (1904); Hammond v. Hyde Park, 195 Mass 29, 80 NE 650 (1907); State ex rel. O'Bannon v. Cole, 220 Mo 697, 119 SW 424 (1909); McSween v. Board of School Trustees of Ft. Worth, 60 TexCivApp 270, 129 SW 206 (1910).

[47] Hutchins v. School Committee of Durham, 137 NC 68, 49 SE 46 (1904).

Challenging a school board rule requiring vaccination, a plaintiff attacked the rule as being an unreasonable exercise of power because, he asserted: (1) there was no epidemic or danger of epidemic in the city; (2) vaccination was not a preventive of smallpox; (3) vaccination was a threat to health and life; and (4) vaccination was in opposition to his conscientious beliefs.[48] The court replied:

> The board of education by its resolution did not undertake or intend to compel the children to be vaccinated. . . . The board only undertook to control the schools under its jurisdiction. The resolution did not prevent the children from attending the schools; it was their own consciences, beliefs, and convictions that did.

Other jurisdictions have made similar rulings declaring it within the power of school boards to adopt health regulations although they were not specifically empowered by the legislature to do so and although no immediate danger existed.[49] A court in Texas upheld the right of a school board to prescribe the method of vaccination to be used to fulfill the requirement.[50] The Supreme Court of Illinois held that a superintendent of schools had exceeded his authority in attempting to exclude an unvaccinated child from school upon his own authority and not upon a rule of the board of education.[51] A Georgia court, four years later, held that an attendance officer was without authority to order the vaccination of children.[52]

§ 5.3 Regulating the attendance of physically or mentally incompetent pupils

Although every state provides a system of free education, the privilege of school attendance is contingent upon the

---

[43] Staffel v. San Antonio School Board of Education, 201 SW 413 (Texas, 1918).

[49] Abney v. Fox, 250 SW 210 (Texas, 1923); Johnson v. Dallas, 291 SW 972 (Texas, 1927); Booth v. Board of Education of Fort Worth Independent School Dist., 70 SW(2d) 350 (Texas, 1934); Pierce v. Board of Education of Fulton, 219 NYS(2d) 519 (1961).

[50] Abney v. Fox, 250 SW 210 (Texas, 1923).

[51] Burroughs v. Mortenson, 312 Ill 163, 143 NW 457 (1924).

[52] Sherman v. Board of Education of Bartow County, 165 Ga 889, 142 SE 152 (1928).

willingness of pupils to subject themselves to such reasonable rules and regulations as may operate in their school district. Failure to abide by these rules, either intentionally or unintentionally, may result in punitive action being taken by local school authorities. In the absence of specific rules, it has been accepted generally that a child who continually disrupts the order and harmony of a class by inappropriate behavior and who upon admonition does not improve his behavior may be excluded from the school until his behavior warrants reinstatement. Since application of these principles seems less difficult in dealing with normal children than with the child physically or mentally handicapped, teachers and parents, through sympathy or lack of recognition of the problem, have permitted severely handicapped children to remain in the classroom to be tolerated or ignored in spite of their behavior or effect upon other pupils.

Few teachers in the public schools have been void of experiences dealing with children who seem to benefit little from instruction but who have a disturbing effect upon other members of the same class or who demand an unproportionate amount of the teacher's time. Fortunately, many school districts have available funds and personnel trained to deal with extreme cases of handicapped children; but even in these areas borderline cases are present and present perplexing problems. Lack of recognition of a child's deficiency, fear of the stigma attached to a child who is "different," or fear of unjust classification has led some parents to insist that their child receive instruction in a regular classroom or, in some cases, has led parents to withdraw their child from school.

When parents or school authorities are dissatisfied with the provisions made for exceptional children, they sometimes call upon the courts to resolve the issues. This section will deal with the rulings of the courts concerning the regulation of school attendance by school authorities of mentally or physically incompetent children. The cases submitted for consideration will be limited to those dealing with incompetency as a major issue, and no attempt will be made to include cases brought to the courts concerning incompetency but whose major issue pertained to pupil placement growing out of segregation issues.

Statements of doctors and teachers were submitted as evidence that a child was "too weak-minded to derive profit from instruction," was "troublesome to other children," and was "unable to take ordinary, decent, physical care of himself."[53] A Massachusetts court sustained the right of the school committee to exclude the child and declared that the facts of the case should not be submitted to a jury for determination:

> Under the law the school committee "have the general charge and superintendence of all the public schools in the town" or city. . . . The management of the schools involves many details; and it is important that a board of public school officers, dealing with these details, and having jurisdiction to regulate the internal affairs of the schools, should not be interfered with or have their conduct called in question before another tribunal, so long as they act in good faith within their jurisdiction. Whether certain acts of disorder so seriously interfere with the school that one who persists in them, either voluntarily or by reason of imbecility, should not be permitted to continue in the school, is a question which the statute makes it their duty to answer: and if they answer honestly, in an effort to do their duty, a jury composed of men of no special fitness to decide educational questions should not be permitted to say that their answer is wrong.

The school committee of Shelburne, Massachusetts, passed a resolution saying that ". . . pupils standing below 60 per cent in two or more subjects shall be demoted one grade, and when such deficiency occurs in the freshman class the delinquent shall be dropped from the roll of the school."[54] A freshman boy fell below the required standard and was not permitted to continue in

---

53 Watson v. Cambridge, 157 Mass 561, 32 NE 864 (1893).
54 Barnard v. Inhabitants of Shelburne, 216 Mass 19, 102 NE 1095 (1913).

school, but he was referred to a teacher of the ninth grade in another school for instruction for the remainder of the school year. The boy remained away from school after his exclusion in December until the following spring. When he presented himself for admittance at his original school, he was refused on the grounds that he still was not prepared to pursue the work there. When action of tort to recover damages for wrongful exclusion was brought, the Supreme Judicial Court of Massachusetts upheld the school committee.[55]

The court ruled:

Although this precise point never has been determined in this commonwealth, it plainly follows, from the general principles by which public schools are governed, and from numerous decisions in which the powers of the school committee to establish reasonable rules and regulations for the government, discipline and general management of the public schools under their charge have been stated with clearness and precision as applicable to a considerable variety of circumstances.

           o   o   o

When the real ground for exclusion from a particular school or grade is failure to maintain a proper standard of scholarship and there is opportunity offered to the pupil to attend another school adapted to his ability and accomplishments, there is no illegal exclusion from school within the meaning of the statute.[56]

The Supreme Court of Wisconsin sustained the expulsion of a child from public school who since his birth had been afflicted with a form of paralysis which affected his use and control of his voice, feet, hands and body.[57] The child had "an uncontrollable flow of saliva" which caused him "to present an unclean appearance." The school board that

---

[55] Barnard v. Inhabitants of Shelburne, 216 Mass 19, 102 NE 1095 (1913); 222 Mass 76, 109 NE 818 (1915).

[56] Barnard v. Inhabitants of Shelburne, 216 Mass 19, 102 NE 1095 (1913).

[57] State ex rel. Beattie v. Board of Education of Antigo, 169 Wis 231, 172 NW 153 (1919).

refused admittance to the child alleged that his presence produced "a depressing and nauseating effect" on the teachers and other children, that he required undue attention from the teacher, and that he annoyed other children.

The court's support of the school committee was explained:

> The duty confronting the school board was a delicate one. It was charged with the responsibility of saying whether this boy should be denied a constitutional right because the exercise of that right would be harmful to the schools and to the pupils attending the same. . . . if his presence in school was detrimental to the best interests of the school, then the board could not, with due regard to their official oaths, refrain from excluding him, even though such action be displeasing and painful to them. The record convinces us that the board took this view of the situation and considered the question with the highest motives and with a full appreciation of its responsibility. There is no suggestion that any of the members were prompted by bad faith or considerations of ill will. The action of the board in refusing to reinstate the boy seems to have been the result of its best judgment, exercised in good faith, and the record discloses no grounds for the interference of courts with its action.

Courts considering the suspension or expulsion of pupils from public school as a result of their mental or physical incompetency sometimes refer to *West* v. *Board of Trustees of Miami University and Miami Normal School,* a case which concerns the expulsion of a pupil in normal school who received grades considered too low by the trustees to justify her continuance in the school program.[58] The Ohio court denied an injunction to the father who sought to restrain the school from carrying out its order to exclude his daughter. That the scholastic standards of the school were within the ability of an average pupil was emphasized

---

[58] West v. Board of Trustees of Miami University and Miami Normal School, 41 OhioApp 367, 181 NE 144 (1931).

by the court, and the court added that ". . . it would not be reasonable to require that the progress of the great body of students, possessing average intellectual development be retarded pending the acquisition by the individual student of the necessary proficiency to proceed."

The Court of Appeals of Ohio affirmed the judgment of a lower court which said that a board of education had not acted within its authority in expelling a child of low mentality from a public school.[59]   A school for retarded children was opened by the school board in 1931, and the Goldman child had been in attendance at school during the 1931-32 and 1932-33 school years.   A resolution adopted by the board of education said, among other statements, that children with an intelligence quotient below fifty would not be permitted to attend the school after a specified date. The school board, relying on test scores to exclude the child, said:

> . . . the department of education of the state can prescribe standards, examinations, or tests by which it may be determined whether or not certain children of school age are incapable of profiting substantially by further instruction in the schools; that these examinations and tests were given to this child and that this child was determined to be of such low mentality as to be incapable of profiting substantially by further instruction in the schools.

The court said that this was the first case of which it had knowledge that ". . . gives the right to exclude from all educational facilities any child within the prescribed ages upon the basis of an intelligence test."   The record of the court showed that results of four intelligence tests taken by the Goldman child between September, 1932, and October, 1933, ranged from 45 to 55; and an examination of the Ohio statutes prompted the court to say that authority to exclude the child rested with the state department of education.

---

[59] Board of Education of Cleveland Heights v. State ex rel. Goldman, 47 OhioApp 417, 191 NE 914 (1934).

A fourteen-year old child who had had infantile paralysis and who suffered "continually from pain" had done unsatisfactory work in school and was assigned to a non-graded school which provided a special program for children who had difficulty in regular school due to physical, mental, or speech defects; but the parents refused to send the child to the assigned school.[60]   The trial court, finding that the school was different from other schools in that it was not graded and that it was not within the school district in which the child resided, declared that the parents were not in violation of the compulsory school law.   The Supreme Court of Iowa noted that the parent had the opportunity of letting his child attend a private school, the special school, or receive private instruction, but that he did none of these. Reversing the judgment of the lower court, the higher court found the parent guilty under the provisions of the compulsory school attendance law and said:

> No claim is made that the child was not in proper physical and mental condition to attend school, nor that the child had been excused from school attendance for sufficient reason by a court of record or judge. While there is here an unhappy and unfortunate situation, yet the uncontroverted facts presented and the provisions the legislature has made left no room for an acquittal.[61]

Another case involving the enforcement of the compulsory school law as applied to children physically or mentally handicapped may be found in Pennsylvania.[62]   A child, eleven years old, was placed by school authorities in a public school for deaf children.   The Wingard child, in the fourth grade before being placed in the special school, annoyed other children on the playground, was sent to the principal's office for a disciplinary conference on the average of once a week, and had to be shouted at in order to hear.   Testimony was presented showing that the child

---

[60] State v. Ghrist, 222 Iowa 1069, 270 NW 376 (1936); 272 NW 440 (1937).
[61] State v. Ghrist, 222 Iowa 1069, 270 NW 376 (1936).
[62] Wingard Petition, 18 Som 1, 7 D&C(2d) 522 (1956).

read on a first grade level and that his other work was "almost negligible." The court record showed that the parents of the child were cooperative but objected to their child's being placed in a school that taught sign language for communication. They withdrew the boy from the special school, and proceedings were instituted against them.

The Pennsylvania court, declaring the child a neglected child, ruled:

> Ordinarily we think of a neglected child as one who is neglected in so far as his physical necessities and comforts are concerned, such as his food, clothing and shelter. These are not the all inclusive considerations, however. Our civilization has advanced to that point where the proper education of a child is a necessity secondary only to that of his food, clothing and shelter if he is to become a man and take his place in a highly competitive and curiously independent society. To fail to provide this necessity today, either willfully, or by neglect omission, may be accounted neglect in the circumstances.

The Supreme Court of New York dismissed the petition of a parent who asked that the courts review the determination of a local board of education to transfer the petitioner's daughter from a school for children with intelligence quotients of not less than 50 to a school for children with an intelligence quotient of less than 50.[63] The board based its determination upon tests given by the school psychologist while the parent presented test scores from a test administered by a hired psychologist. The New York court reversed the earlier judgment[64] of the Supreme Court of Special Term by saying that the determination of the matter should be reviewed by the commissioner of education of New York and not by the courts.[65] At the time of this writing no further disposition of the case has been reported.

A New Jersey statute provided for the education and training of subnormal and physically handicapped children;

---

63 Realy v. Caine, 220 NYS(2d) 857 (1961); In re Realy v. Caine, 230 NYS(2d) 453 (1962).
64 Realy v. Caine, 220 NYS(2d) 857 (1961).
65 In re Realy v. Caine, 230 NYS(2d) 453 (1962).

and when the parents and school authorities disagreed as to a child's classification, the court ruled that the board of education was "duty-bound" to provide facilities for all children within the classification of trainable and educable.[66] When the investigation of the court revealed the child to be a borderline case, the court recommended that the child be given another trial in the educable classification; but the court, relying upon the judgment of experts, informed the parents that the child was not ready for the speech therapy which they sought.

§ 5.4 Enforcing other regulations pertaining to health

With the responsibility for managing the nation's schools goes a responsibility for the welfare of the children enrolled in those schools. That one could find in any state constitutional provisions or statutory enactments prescribing the control to be employed by the school in all instances pertaining to the health of its pupils would not be expected. As large numbers of people assemble, the possibilities of contracting communicable and infectious diseases are increased. The school concerned with the welfare of the individual as well as the group must weigh carefully its plan for eliminating threats to the health of others posed by the presence of an ill child in the classroom.

The concern for the health of school children and the community has led school boards and health boards in many communities to work cooperatively for prevention of disease and promotion of health; but when differences of opinion concerning the authority to close school or to deny admission to children have existed, the courts in some instances have been asked to serve as mediators. The decision of when a child's presence becomes detrimental to the well-being of the members in his school and the decision when he, for his own good or for the good of others, must be excluded from school sometimes provokes questions of a legal nature which may be resolved only in the courtroom.

When an epidemic of Spanish influenza threatened a city, the local board of health adopted a rule against congregating

---

[66] Exposito v. Barber, 74 NJSuper 289, 181 A(2d) 201 (1961).

in public places; and under this rule it ordered the schools of the city to be closed. The school district maintained that passage and enforcement of such a rule was unreasonable and beyond the authority and jurisdiction of the board of health. The Supreme Court of Arizona said that the action taken by the health board was an emergency measure taken to prevent the spread of disease and would remain in effect until the emergency passed.[67]

The words of the court were:

> While school trustees and educational administrative officers are vested with power to establish, provide for, govern, and regulate public schools within their jurisdictions, they are in these respects nowise subject to the direction or control of the state or county or city boards of health, yet when the necessity arises to close the schools for the protection of the public health such emergency, while it exists, is a superior power to that given school administration officers, and the law of necessity controls the situation during the existence of the emergency giving rise to the power.

The Supreme Court of Oregon in *Crane* v. *School Dist. No. 14 of Tillamook County* considered the case of a school bus driver who was denied his salary during the period of time when the schools closed as a result of an epidemic of influenza.[68] In awarding the judgment to the bus driver, the court upheld the school board in its right to close the public schools:

> Under the general powers of control and supervision, the closing of school for any reason rests in the sound discretion of the school board, and therefore is not a question of law. The Legislature has rightfully assumed that in all such matters the school boards will work in harmony with the boards of health to prevent, suppress,

---

[67] Globe School Dist. No. 1 of Globe v. Board of Health of Globe, 20 Ariz 208, 179 Pac 55 (1919).

[68] Crane v. School Dist. No. 14 of Tillamook County, 95 Ore 644, 188 Pac 712 (1920).

control, and regulate the existence and spread of contagious diseases.

Learning that a county had been found to have 120 cases
of trachoma and 350 suspected cases, the Supreme Court of
North Dakota in *Martin* v. *Craig* upheld the order of the
county board of health which required school officials to
deny admission to the public schools any children who were
known to have or suspected of having the disease.[69] The
school authorities refused admission to two children in
the same family when one was said by a health official to
have trachoma, a disease which is communicable and often
results in blindness.   When two other doctors testified
that the child was not affected with trachoma, Martin, the
father, petitioned the court for a preemptory writ to compel
the admission of his children to the school. The seriousness
of the disease and the ease with which it spreads prompted
the court to rule in favor of the authorities although some
doubt existed as to whether the children in the immediate
case were affected.

Margaret Stone, a six-year old child, was found to have
a throat infection and was excluded from attendance at a
public school. She was told by the school authorities that
she would be readmitted upon the presentation of a "negative report from a throat culture submitted to the division
of public health of the city" and a certificate from a physician. The father refused to follow the instructions of
the school officials on the basis of his conscientious
objections to medical treatment, and he brought action
against the school board to have his daughter readmitted
to the public schools.[70] The Supreme Court of Minnesota
pointed out that the protection of the health of the children in the charge of the school was one of its primary
duties and that "all authority exercised in the protection
of the public health is to be liberally construed." The court
concluded that the rule was made in good faith, was not
unfair or arbitrary, and was not unreasonable. The court
further stated:

---

69 Martin v. Craig, 42 ND 213, 173 NW 787 (1919).
70 Stone v. Probst, 165 Minn 361, 206 NW 642 (1925).

Many of us may have to subordinate our own ideas or views to governmental authority, and the requirement calls for co-operation without requiring any one to surrender his own views or conscientious objection thereto. The child is required to remain away if he will not submit to the rule. The board asks only for such information as it deems necessary in the proper administration of the schools. This information would result in exclusion only in the event the child himself was a menace to his associates. The board provides a way for the child to qualify for admission without any cost or expense. The matter is entirely in his own hands.

Five children were suspended from the public schools of Dighton, Massachusetts; and when the father requested the reasons for suspension in writing from the school committee, he was told that his children were sent home until they could rid themselves of head lice. The children were returned to school about one month later only to be sent home again after an examination by the school physician and superintendent showed the children not "in a proper condition to attend school." Carr, the father of the children, requested a hearing be held by the school committee to "ratify or disapprove" of the action that had been taken by the superintendent and principal of the school. A hearing was not held, and the children did not return to school. The father, in his request for a hearing, had alleged that the school physician had not acted in good faith, that the superintendent had failed "to afford him the promised protection," and that only three of the five children excluded were examined. Ruling in favor of the plaintiff, the Supreme Judicial Court of Massachusetts said that the school committee had been given the general charge and superintendence of the school, but failure to grant the requested hearing would indicate that the exclusion of the five children was not made in good faith.[71]

Further discussing the broad powers of the school committee, the court said:

---

[71] Carr v. Inhabitants of Dighton, 229 Mass 304, 118 NE 525 (1918).

In the exercise of these broad powers their decision, involving the exercise of judgment and discretion, is not reviewable by the courts when they act in good faith in determining the facts on which that decision is based. . . . And in this case, if the committee had given the plaintiffs a fair and impartial hearing, admittedly their decision would have been final.

A resolution adopted by a school board requiring each pupil at the beginning of the school year to have a physical examination was upheld by the Supreme Court of South Dakota in *Streich* v. *Board of Education of Independent School Dist. of Aberdeen.*[72] Streich charged the school board with adding to the qualifications prescribed by law for admission and attendance to public schools. The school board said it had adopted the rule to protect the community and pupils from the spread of contagious diseases and to help understand the health of children in order to make allowances for any physical deficiencies which might be discovered. Testimony was presented to show that the general health of the school had improved since the adoption of the rule.

Streich said that the physical examination in itself was an invasion of personal rights and could make suggestions which would result in "mental disease germs." The court answered the allegations by Streich:

Appellant urges that respondents were adding to the qualifications for admission prescribed by law. There is no merit in this contention; one might as well contend that to require a pupil to take his term examination to ascertain his progress in school work was the adding of a qualification for membership in the school. Under the regulation complained of, no person is excluded from the school, except upon his volition.

* * *

The established customs—the conventionalities of the time—are matters to be considered in determining the rea-

72 Streich v. Board of Education of Independent School Dist. of Aberdeen, 34 SD 169, 147 NW 779 (1914).

sonableness of a particular action; therefore a thing may be reasonable though it conflicts with the individual views of the few, if it conforms to that of many. Such an examination as the report calls for could not subject a child to anything not in perfect harmony with the conventions of to-day, could not subject it to indignity, and would be reasonable.

     ✿   ✿   ✿

If such an examination is a menace to a child's health owing to the danger of mental suggestion, the study of physiology and hygiene should be banished from our schools. The time may come when the contentions of the appellant will become the accepted doctrine of the day, but courts must follow the accepted doctrine of the present, except when, through competent evidence submitted, the fallacy of a particular doctrine is established.

An Ohio court declared reasonable a resolution by a school board which provided for the withdrawal of any pupil from school upon the knowledge of pregnancy.[73] In rendering its judgment, the court gave special consideration to the school board's attempt to provide special lessons to the suspended pupil, its expressed interest in the pregnant pupil's physical well-being, and its concern for the welfare of other pupils and the school in general.

§ 5.5 Summary

The recognition that good health is important to school achievement, the realization that the presence of an ill child in a classroom may adversely affect the achievement of other class members, and the desire to prevent the spread of disease and to promote good health have prompted schools over the country to adopt health programs designed to protect and improve the health of the pupils in their charge. Familiarization with the various school health programs or review of a listing of the services offered by the public school will probably lead one to subscribe to the supposition that the concept of school health services has

---

[73] Ohio ex rel. Idle v. Chamberlain, supra, § 3.3, n 23.

broadened greatly since the turn of the century. While many express satisfaction with the health services provided by the school, some clamor for additional services, and still others challenge the authority of the school to venture into the area of health. During the past seventy years few areas of pupil control have demanded the attention of the various tribunals as often as has the area of health.

Among the most numerous and the earliest cases involving health were those dealing with vaccination. The courts have been in one accord in ruling that it is within the power of the legislature, boards of health, agencies of the city, or boards of education to enact rules and regulations requiring vaccination as a condition of school attendance if known cases of smallpox exist or if an epidemic threatens. In spite of the conscientious objections of an individual, the fear of physical danger involved in vaccination, or disbelief in the effectiveness of vaccination as a preventive of smallpox, the courts, emphasizing the necessity for relinquishing personal beliefs for the welfare of many, have upheld the legislatures in various states in enacting statutes requiring vaccination and have called upon school boards to enforce the legislative provisions. The court has found no conflict between the compulsory school attendance law and the vaccination legislation; and, furthermore, in *Lee* v. *Marsh, supra,* § 5.2, n 4 and 9, it has upheld the legislature in prescribing the method of vaccination to be employed. When a school board was challenged to provide free education for an unvaccinated child excluded from the public schools, the court in *State ex rel. Dunham* v. *Board of Education of City School Dist. of Cincinnati, supra,* § 5.2, nn 4, 9, ruled that the child was denied a free education by his own volition and that the responsibility of the school board was fulfilled through furnishing the public schools for those who abide by its rules and regulations. When the courts were confronted by the federal question concerning an invasion of rights guaranteed by the United States Constitution, they found support in *Jacobson* v. *Commonwealth of Massachusetts, supra,* § 5.2, n 14, in which the Supreme Court of the United States upheld a statute permitting cities to require vaccination of all their inhabitants.

Without exception, when emergency measures have been prescribed, the courts have upheld the orders of boards of health and city councils which require school authorities to refuse admission in the public schools to unvaccinated children. School boards, who usually have been given general control and superintendence of schools, have been placed in a subordinate position to boards of health in the presence of an immediate danger to the community welfare. In an emergency not only may boards of health require vaccination for school admittance, but the courts have also placed it within their authority to prescribe the method to be used in vaccination and to close the schools if they deemed it necessary to prevent the spread of disease. In the absence of an epidemic the courts are not of one opinion concerning the authority of boards of health to prescribe health measures dealing with school admittance. While some jurisdictions uphold the boards of health in adopting rules requiring vaccination, others define the duties of the health authorities as being administrative rather than legislative.

School boards in the absence of specific statutory authority have depended upon their discretionary power to enact rules requiring vaccination, and in the instance of an emergency the courts have upheld their action. Some question remains as to whether school boards possess such authority in the absence of a threat to the health of the pupils; but when they have been upheld in their authority, the court has held in *Allen* v. *Ingalls, supra*, § 5.2, n 37, that they may refuse to admit children who have been vaccinated by the homeopathic method. A rule to be considered reasonable and subject to enforcement must be made by the school board and not by a superintendent, *Burroughs* v. *Mortenson, supra*, § 5.2, n 51, or an attendance officer, *Sherman* v. *Board of Education of Bartow County, supra*, § 5.2, n 52.

Most school authorities at some time have been placed in a position to weigh their responsibility for one child in relation to their responsibility for the education of all children. Particularly is this consideration necessary in dealing with children who have serious physical or mental handicaps and who wish to attend the regular classes of the public schools. The courts have been asked in several instances to resolve the differences resulting from the determination made by those charged with the responsibility for educating the youth of a community.

A Massachusetts court in *Watson v. Cambridge, supra,* § 5.3, n 53, sustained the authority of the school committee to exclude a child who was "too weak-minded to derive profit from instruction" and who created an undue number of problems for the teachers and other pupils. A few years later a school committee in Shelbourne, Massachusetts, passed a resolution which provided for the exclusion of pupils who fell below a required standard in their studies; and when a freshman boy was denied admission to a public school under the provisions of the rule, his father sought satisfaction in the courts. Since the child had been afforded an opportunity to go to a school better "adapted to his ability and accomplishments" the court in *Barnard v. Inhabitants of Shelbourne, supra,* § 5.3, nn 54-56, found nothing illegal in his expulsion.

A child who was afflicted with a form of paralysis which affected his use and control of his voice, hands, feet, and body and who had a "depressing and nauseating effect" on teachers and pupils was excluded from the public schools of Antigo. The board was thought by the court, *Beattie v. Board of Education of Antigo, supra,* § 5.3, n 57, to have acted "with highest motives and with a full appreciation of its responsibility" and was, therefore, within its authority to exclude the child from the school.

An Ohio court in *West v. Board of Trustees of Miami Univ. and Miami Normal School, supra,* § 5.3, n 58, denied injunctive relief to a father who sought to restrain the normal school from carrying out its order to exclude his daughter for her failure to maintain the scholastic standard required by the school. Three years later in *Board of Edu-*

cation of Cleveland Heights v. *State ex rel. Goldman, supra,* § 5.3, n 59, the Court of Appeals of Ohio said that a board of education had not acted within its authority in expelling a child of low mentality from a public school for retarded children on the sole basis of his low scores on intelligence tests.

When a special school for physically or mentally handicapped children is provided and a child has been assigned to the school, parents may be found in violation of the compulsory school attendance law if they refuse to permit their child to attend the school. A fourteen-year old child was assigned to a school which provided a special program for children who had difficulty in regular school due to physical, mental, or speech defects; but his parents refused to send the child to the assigned school. The Supreme Court of Iowa, *State* v. *Ghrist, supra,* § 5.3, nn 60, 61, pointed out that the parents could have sent their child to the special school, a private school, or provided private instruction. Their failure to provide their child with instruction by any of these alternatives led the court to find them guilty under the provisions of the compulsory school attendance law. A similar disposition of a case was made by a Pennsylvania court in the *Wingard Petition, supra,* § 5.3, n 62, when parents refused to send their deaf child to an assigned school because of their objection to his learning sign language.

The Supreme Court of New York, in *In re Realy* v. *Caine, supra,* § 5.3, nn 63-65, dismissed the petition of a parent who asked that the court review the determination of a local board of education to transfer the petitioner's daughter from a class for the educable to a class for the trainable. The New York court ruled that the determination of the matter should be reviewed by the New York commissioner of education and not by the court. A case of similar circumstances may be found in *Exposito* v. *Barber, supra,* § 5.3, n 66. The New Jersey court disposed of the case by recommending that the school board give the child involved another trial before placing her in the lower intelligence grouping since she seemed to be a borderline case.

Attempting to protect other students, some school boards have found it necessary to exclude children whose health might endanger the health of others or whose presence might have a detrimental effect upon the discipline and well-being of the school. Although a school board did not see the necessity for such action, a local board of health ordered the schools closed when an epidemic of influenza threatened a city. The school board charged the health board with taking action which was unreasonable and beyond its authority, but the Supreme Court of Arizona in *Globe School Dist. No. 1 of Globe* v. *Board of Health of Globe, supra,* § 5.4, n 67, upheld the emergency measure taken to prevent the spread of disease. Another case which gives some insight into the authority to close schools is *Crane* v. *School Dist. No. 14 of Tillamook County, supra,* § 5.4, n 68. This case dealt with the request of a bus driver for salary during a period when schools were closed because of an epidemic. The court in making its judgment declared that the school board was within its authority to close schools when it felt the necessity.

When the school authorities refused admittance to two children who were suspected of having trachoma, the seriousness of the illness led the Supreme Court of South Dakota in *Martin* v. *Craig, supra,* § 5.4, n 69, to rule in favor of the school authorities although some doubt existed as to whether the excluded children were infected with the disease. Considering protection of health one of the primary duties of the school, a Minnesota court in *Stone* v. *Probst, supra,* § 5.4, n 70, declared reasonable a rule which excluded a child with a sore throat until a certificate from a doctor and a "negative report" were submitted to the school authorities.

When a school board does not act in good faith in carrying out its duties, it cannot expect the support of the courts. The refusal of a school board to grant a hearing requested by a father was the sole reason given in *Carr* v. *Inhabitants of Dighton, supra,* § 5.4, n 71, by the court for not upholding the exclusion of children who were found to have head lice.

A resolution requiring pupils to have a physical examination at the beginning of the school year was upheld by the Supreme Court of South Dakota in *Streich* v. *Board of Education of Independent School Dist. of Aberdeen, supra,* § 5.4, n 72. The court gave much weight to the arguments of the school board that the examination was required to help prevent the spread of disease and to furnish information that would be helpful in making provisions for children with health problems.

An Ohio court in *Ohio ex rel. Idle* v. *Chamberlain, supra,* § 5.4, n 73, declared reasonable the exclusion of a pregnant pupil from the public schools. Of influence to the court in making its judgment was the apparent concern by the school board for the health and welfare of the girl as well as for her fellow pupils.

The authority of school officials to adopt rules and regulations pertaining to health has been challenged frequently. As new demands are made of the school and as school systems throughout the country strive to protect and promote good health among their pupils and their community, it is likely that new challenges to the authority of the school in health areas will arise. The judicial decisions thus far reported may furnish some insight into the determination that will be made by the courts when new cases arise and may enable the school person to anticipate the possible outcome of the action which he is planning.

Chapter 6

LEGAL CONSIDERATIONS IN THE CONTROL
OF CERTAIN TYPES OF WILLFUL
MISCONDUCT

Written contributions which supplement or restate the ideas found in the already voluminous store of literature concerning the control and management of children in a school situation are published regularly, and there seems to be no indication that suggestions for securing and maintaining an orderly classroom or school campus will cease in the years to come. With the concern that has been expressed and the articles and books that have been written on the subject, one might think that all questions relating to the discipline of pupils would have been answered and that each school would have achieved the order which it desires by heeding the advice or following the prescriptions of the various writers, but few gatherings of educators are held when the problem of discipline is not discussed.

§ 6.1 Discipline, an unsolved problem

The complexity of the problem in itself aggravated by the inability to predict or foresee every act of misbehavior has rendered discipline a problem which demands much time and energy. As many new teachers join the profession, they seek the advice of other teachers in their dealings with pupils and often expect to be given a formula which may be applied to all situations—a formula that those experienced in dealing with pupils are unable to provide. Wise exercise of discretion, reliance upon professional advice, and knowledge of what is appropriate educationally, ethically, and legally in dealing with pupil misbehavior will help the wary teacher to avoid making many mistakes in judgment that might be harmful to the pupils, the teaching profession, and her career.

In each of the fifty states may be found constitutional provisions for educating the youth of the state and legislative enactments which designate boards of education legally constituted bodies to operate and manage the public schools. The power of school authorities to control the pupils within their charge is for the most part derived from their discretionary grant of power which gives them the right and authority to make and enforce reasonable rules and regulations for the good government, good order, and efficient operation of the schools and is limited only by constitutional provisions, statutory enactments, and judicial interpretations of the laws. That the framers of the various state constitutions or the members of the state legislatures might provide specific language defining the extent of control to be exerted by school authorities in all situations for all times is inconceivable; for this reason, if no other, judicial interpretation of the existing laws holds an important place in the public school system.

Although few school officials would endeavor to enforce rules for the orderly conduct of the school to the limits sanctioned by law, judicial decisions may provide the legal framework for the formulation of policies regarding discipline of pupils. Court decisions ultimately set the boundaries as to extent of control which may be exerted by school authorities and provide legal principles to guide the actions of teachers, administrators, and school board members in planning for the welfare of individual pupils and for the school.

The courts considering diverse cases involving the legal exercise of control over pupils have ruled:

In accordance with the broadly stated rule that the exclusive control of methods of discipline is in teachers, principals, and superintendents, such control is said not to be within the power of a school board. As a general rule, however, the school board which by statute has the general charge and superintendence of the public schools has power to adopt appropriate and reasonable rules and regulations for the discipline and management of such schools, such as a rule requiring that there shall be prompt attendance, diligence in study, and proper deportment. The decision of such board, if exercised in good faith, on matters affecting the good order and discipline of the school is final as far as it relates to the rights of pupils to enjoy school privileges, and the courts will not interfere with the exercise of such authority unless it has been illegally or unreasonably exercised; but the courts will interfere to prevent the enforcement of a rule which deprives a pupil of rights to which the law entitles him, or which tends to alienate the pupil from proper parental authority, or which manifestly reaches beyond the school board's power, or beyond its sphere of action, and relates to subjects in no way connected with the management or successful operation of the school, or which is plainly calculated to subvert or retard the leading object of the school legislation of the state.[1]

Without a doubt school authorities have been given broad discretionary powers in administering the school program and in maintaining the order and good conduct necessary in the best interest of the schools, but in the exercise of discretion it would be rare to find universal approval of any action taken. Extreme cases of disapproval which have resulted in litigation may produce information which will be helpful to others in determining the position of the court regarding the reasonableness and legality of the measures they employ to regulate the conduct of the pupils for whom they are responsible. Since even a listing of possible instances of willful misconduct contemplated or perpetrated by imaginative pupils would be exhaustless, the writer has chosen to investigate the ruling of the courts in three areas of misconduct which may prove to be of interest to school boards and administrators;

---

[1] "Schools and School Districts," Corpus Juris Secundum, 79 (Brooklyn, New York: The American Law Book Company, 1952), p. 443.

the research presented deals with damage to school property, public criticism or ridicule of the school, and leaving the school campus during school hours.

§ 6.2 Authority of school officials to hold pupils responsible for damage to school property

Millions of dollars are spent each year by school districts in the United States to repair or to replace property damaged or destroyed accidentally, willfully, or maliciously by pupils. Some of the expense is incurred by the thoughtless or careless acts of boys and girls attending the schools, but much of the damage is not a result of accidental breakage or defacement; it has been done intentionally by pupils expressing their ill feelings toward the schools or some particular aspects of school life, or destruction has been done maliciously and wantonly by individuals or gangs seeking a thrill or deriving pleasure from the act of destroying the property of others. When pupils have been discovered destroying school property, teachers and administrators in many areas have punished the offenders or required them to pay for the damage that had been done.

In 1961 it was reported that the cost of replacing broken glass in the cities of Chicago, Baltimore, and Minneapolis was in excess of a quarter of a million dollars.[2] The cost of vandalism in some cities has risen so steadily in the past few years that the amount being expended could be used to build additional classrooms, hire more teachers, or build a new school building.[3] The problem of what to do to protect the property for which the school board holds statutory responsibility has led school officers to employ night watchmen to discourage intruders, to build fences to make access to the buildings more difficult, or to install electronic security devices to frighten trespassers or summon police officers when unauthorized persons enter the buildings. Many administrators urge the passage of laws which hold parents liable for damage to property inflicted by their children willfully or maliciously. In response to

---

[2] Tom Probst, "How To Cut Down Vandalism," The Nation's Schools, LXVIII (September, 1961), p. 64.
[3] Ibid., p. 100.

the demands that parents be made liable for the restructive acts of their children, almost half of the states have enacted some type of legislation since 1955 concerning parental responsibility for acts of vandalism.[4] The number of instances in which these statutes have been enforced is unknown. A North Carolina statute which holds parents liable to the extent of $500 for acts of vandalism done by their children to the property of others was adjudicated as late as 1963.[5] Undoubedly other cases resulting from the enforcement of the parent responsibility laws have appeared and been resolved in the lower courts, but the final test of the constitutionality of such laws will be found in the higher courts.

In 1880 the Supreme Court of Iowa in *Perkins v. Board of Directors of the Independent School Dist. of West Des Moines* reviewed the circumstances of the first case brought to the higher courts involving pupil responsibility for damage to school property.[6] A boy, twelve years old, broke a window in a school while he was playing ball in a nearby field. Upon being asked to pay the damages amounting to three dollars, the boy indicated he was unable to pay. The school board had enacted a rule to the effect that any pupil damaging school property must pay the damages incurred or be excluded from school. When confronted with the rule and the necessity of payment by the school authorities, the parents of the boy refused to pay for the damage. The superintendent, supported in his position by the board, denied the boy further admittance to the school until payment was made.

Reversing the judgment of the lower court, the Supreme Court of Iowa ruled against the regulation adopted by the board of directors of the school district, and Judge Beck said:

---

[4] James Colmey and Thomas Valentine, "Stop Vandalism with Parent Responsibility Laws," The American School Board Journal, CXLI (July, 1960), p. 9.

[5] "Vandalism Claim Rejected by Court," The News and Observer (Raleigh), CXCV, No. CXLIV (November 21, 1962), p. 20.

[6] Perkins v. Board of Directors of the Independent School Dist. of West Des Moines, 56 Iowa 476, 9 NW 356 (1880).

It will be observed that plaintiff was guilty of no breach of discipline or of any offense against good order. By an accident and without an evil purpose he broke a window glass. . . . We may admit that he ought to pay the damages, and is liable therefor; but we think his omission to perform this duty cannot be punished by expulsion from the school. The state does not deprive its citizens of their property or their liberty, or of any right, except as a punishment for a crime. It would be very harsh and obviously unjust to deprive a child of education for the reason that through accident and without intention of wrong he destroyed property of the school-district. Doubtless a child may be expelled from school as a punishment for breach of discipline, or for offense against good morals but not for innocent acts. In this case the plaintiff was expelled, not because he broke the glass, but because he did not pay the damage sustained by the breaking. . . . The rule requiring him to make payment is not intended to secure good order, but to enforce an obligation to pay a sum of money. We are clearly of the opinion that the directors have no authority to promulgate or enforce such a rule.

The Supreme Court of Indiana when confronted by a similar case reasoned that although a ". . . teacher has the right to exact from pupils obedience to his lawful and reasonable demands and rules, and to punish for disobedience . . . .," he may be found guilty of assault and battery when he attempts to enforce by chastisement a rule which requires pupils to "pay for the wanton and careless destruction of school property."[7] Declaring such a rule unreasonable, the court emphasized that carelessness is a characteristic found in most children and that the inability of a child to pay for damage resulting from such carelessness should not subject him to punishment. Ruling thus, the court explained:

Carelessness on the part of children is one of the most common, and yet one of the least blameworthy, of their

---

[7] State v. Vanderbilt, 116 Ind 11, 18 NE 266 (1888).

faults. In simple carelessness there is no purpose to do wrong. To punish a child for carelessness, in any case, is to punish it when it has no purpose or intent to do wrong, or violate rules. But beyond this, no rule is reasonable which requires of the pupils what they cannot do. The vast majority of pupils, whether small or large, have no money at their command with which to pay for school property which they injure or destroy by carelessness or otherwise. If required to pay for such property, they would have to look to their parents or guardians for the money. If the parent or guardian should not have the money, or if they should refuse to give it to the child, the child would be left subject to punishment for not having done what it had no power to do.

In the case of *Holman* v. *School Trustees of Avon* a father sought the reinstatement of his son who had been suspended from a public school under the provisions of a rule adopted by the school district which stated, "Pupils who shall, in any way, deface or injure the school building, outhouses, furniture, maps, or anything else belonging to the school, shall be suspended from school until full satisfaction is made."[8] The ten-year old son of the plaintiff "negligently and carelessly" had broken a windowpane in the schoolhouse; and when the father refused to pay one dollar for the damage done by his son, the boy was suspended from school. The father applied for the readmission of his son to school, but he was informed by the teacher and school directors that the child would not be readmitted until damages were paid or the window was replaced.

The Supreme Court of Michigan saw in the enforcement of such a rule the possibility that some children would be denied the opportunity of an education through a careless or negligent act committed "without malice or willfulness." Although the sum of money involved in the immediate case could be paid "without serious financial detriment" and would have been less expensive than court action, the father decided "to stand upon his rights" and by so doing

---

[8] Holman v. School Trustees of Avon, 77 Mich 605, 43 NW 996 (1889).

provided the courts with an opportunity to rule upon the authority and power of boards of education to enforce a rule such as the one in question and thereby deprive some children of the benefits of the public schools of the state. The Michigan court refused to uphold the school directors in the enforcement of the rule and issued a writ ordering the reinstatement of the child who had been wrongfully excluded from school.

The South Dakota statute which provided, "Any pupil, who cuts, defaces, or otherwise injures any schoolhouse, apparatus, or outbuilding thereof, is liable to suspension or expulsion, and, on the complaint of the teacher to any member of the school board, the parents or guardians of such pupil shall be liable for all damages," was tested in the highest court of the state.[9] A school district brought action to recover damages from the parents of a boy who had intentionally injured school property. The boy, sixteen years old and a pupil in the school, entered a school building with another boy; and while they were there, they adjusted the drinking fountain so as to make it overflow and then threw cement on the floors of the building. When the building was opened the following morning, considerable damage was found. With all judges concurring, the Supreme Court of South Dakota dismissed the petition against the parents because of certain statutory provisions.

Since South Dakota had a general law which stated that neither parent nor child is answerable as such, for the act of the other," the statute which established parental responsibility for damages to school property was examined closely by the court before it made the statement:

> We cannot assume that the words "on the complaint of the teacher" were put in the statute without some legislative purpose. It seems the words have no purpose when the damage was committed at a time when the teacher had no more knowledge concerning the cause of damage than a member of the school board or anyone else. The words disclose a definite purpose when the

---

9 Lamro Independent Consol. School Dist. No. 20 of Tripp County v. Cawthorne, 76 SD 106, 73 NW(2d) 337 (1955).

application of the statute is limited to the time the child is under the immediate supervision of the teacher, and we do not believe the language of the statute should be further extended. In any event making liability of parents dependent upon a complaint of the teacher makes it appear extremely doubtful whether the legislature intended that such liability should exist for acts of the child when not under the immediate supervision of the teacher, and applying the above rule of statutory construction, we must hold that the general law on the subject applies and the parents are not answerable for the acts of the child under the circumstances here presented.

Four years later a New Jersey court rendered a judgment in favor of a school board that sought to recover damages from the parents of a boy who had purposely set fire to a school building.[10] The defendants' son and another pupil enrolled in the Palmyra High School went to the high school on a Sunday night for the alleged purpose of getting some examination papers. The school board charged the Hansen boy with setting fire to the school while he was there and thus causing damages to the extent of $344,000. The board of education brought its suit under the parent responsibility law in New Jersey which stated:

> Any pupil who shall cut, deface, or otherwise injure any schoolhouse, furniture, fences, outbuildings, or other property of the school district shall be liable to suspension and punishment, and his parents or guardian shall be liable for damages to the amount of the injury to be collected by the board of education in any court having jurisdiction, together with the costs of action.

In answering the counsel's for defense claim that the statute applied only during school hours, the court said:

> . . . if the Legislature has the right to confer benefits on the people by way of a free education, it certainly has the right to set up the conditions under which such

---

10 Board of Education of Palmyra in County of Burlington v. Hansen, 56 NJSuper 567, 153 A(2d) 393 (1959).

benefits shall be provided. The Legislature has authority to impose restrictions on those seeking to attend the public schools and can suspend or expel for events happening out of school hours. . . .

The New Jersey court further pointed out that parents who wished to exempt themselves from the provisions of statutes applying to public schools could do so by choosing to send their child to a private educational institution. The argument was presented that the statute was unconstitutional in that it unfairly imposed extreme liability upon the parents for acts which they did not commit. The court replied:

> This reasoning touches on equity and moral philosophy. I think it can best be answered by raising this question: Would it be fair to impose the loss on all the other parents of students attending the same school, or upon local tax payers? Suppose, for example, the defendant pupil were to have gone into the school and carved the name "David" on the teacher's desk, and subsequently it cost $50 to repair the damage, and there are 499 other students in the school. Would it be morally just to assess the parents of each ten cents rather than to assess the full amount against the parents of the culprit? If it would be unfair to assess the parents of the wrong doers, how could it be fair to assess the parents of the other 499 innocent students? And yet, if we were to follow the reasoning of the defense counsel, this in substance is what would happen. The parents of the other 499 students (and taxpayers) would each be assessed indirectly for the damages of the tort-feasor. How can it be logically said that it is fair to assess damages against parents of innocent students and taxpayers, unless it be reasoned that in the sharing of the loss by the many there will be less individual hardship and financial stress. This would exemplify charity and not justice.

The Supreme Court of North Carolina in *General Ins. Co. of America* v. *Faulkner* reversed the decision of a lower court when it upheld the application of the North Carolina statute which read:

> . . . Any person, firm, corporation, the State of North Carolina or any political subdivision thereof, or any religious, educational or charitable organization or any nonprofit cemetery corporation, or organization, whether incorporated or unincorporated, shall be entitled to recover damages in an amount not to exceed five hundred dollars ($500.00), in an action in a court of competent jurisdiction, from the parents of any minor under the age of eighteen (18) years, living with its parents, who shall maliciously or willfully destroy property, real, personal or mixed, belonging to such person, firm, corporation, the State of North Carolina or any political subdivision thereof, or any religious, educational or charitable organization.[11]

An elementary school boy entered the auditorium of a public school and "maliciously and willfully" set fire to the draperies causing damages to the building to the amount of $2,916.50. The amount of damage was paid by the company that insured the school; but in turn, the insurance company brought suit against the parents under the provisions of the above stated statute. In rendering its decision, the court pointed out that 31 other states had similar statutes and that the statute was within the police power of the state.

When the question was posed as to parental liability in face of insurance coverage for the damages, the court reasoned:

> We cannot accept the narrow and niggardly interpretation of G. S. 1-538.1 as contended for by defendants. That interpretation would lead to the illogical result that the defendants admittedly liable according to the admissions made by the demurrer for damages to the property of the Kinston City Board of Education in an amount not exceeding $500.00 if it had no insurance,

---

[11] General Ins. Co. of America v. Faulkner, 259 NC 317 (1963).

are relieved of all liability by reason of the collection of
insurance by the Kinston City Board of Education;
in other words, the defendants would receive the
benefit of the insurance without having to pay a cent
for it. . . . it is not apparent why the prudent fore-
sight of the Kinston City Board of Education in protecting
its property by insurance should result in a detriment
to the insurance company who paid the fire loss in full.

§ 6.3 Authority of school officials to punish pupils who publicly criticize or ridicule the school

Since the close of World War II, perhaps more than
any other time in the history of education in the United
States, the public schools have been the recipient of criticism
from lay persons as well as experts. Gaining courage from
those who make open charges against the program, management, or personnel of the school and following the
natural inclination of pupils to complain about their lot,
young people of school age who become disturbed by an
injustice, imagined or real, that has occurred, who object
to a school policy that may in some degree infringe upon
their personal liberties, or who actually seek to improve their
school by suggesting alternatives to existing practices
publicly display their grievances through various media.
Confronted by pupil behavior which they consider insubordination or which they feel may incite other pupils to
similar expressions, teachers and administrators often resort
to employing punitive measures as a defense against further
demonstrations. If the authority of teachers, administrators,
or school board members to control the speech or other
expressions of pupils outside of the classrooms were to be
challenged, undoubtedly, the courts would place some limits
upon the restraints that could be exercised. Although few
sets of circumstances could be expected to be the same,
a review of the decisions made by the courts in cases
dealing with the authority of school officials to punish
pupils who publicly criticize or ridicule the school may
help one to understand the reasoning of the courts.

The first case involving the punishment of a pupil who ridiculed a teacher publicly was considered by the Supreme Court of Vermont over a century ago.[12] An eleven-year old boy was driving his cow by a teacher's house when he, in the presence of other pupils, called the teacher "old Jack Seaver." The next morning when the boy arrived at school he was reprimanded and whipped for his use of "insulting language." The father of the boy insisted that the teacher had no authority to punish the child for an act committed out of and away from school, but the court did not uphold him in his contentions. The reasoning of the court was that since the boy was in the presence of other pupils, his "contemptuous language" had ". . . a direct and immediate tendency to injure the school, to subvert the master's authority, and to beget disorder and insubordination."

The Supreme Court of Iowa in *Murphy* v. *Board of Directors of Independent Dist. of Marengo* issued a writ of mandamus to compel the board of directors of the school district to admit to the public schools a pupil who had been excluded for writing articles ridiculing the board of directors.[13] Some members of the board had visited in a school and after their visit had commented on the lessons that they had observed. Shortly after the visit a pupil wrote and had published two articles which the board claimed were ". . . impertinent, impudent and scandalous, and tended to injure and impair the influence and control of the said board over the said school, as is accorded it by law. . . ." Determining that the articles were creating insubordination in the school and inciting disregard for the authority of the board among other pupils, the board of directors informed the offender that he would be excluded from school until he made a proper, public apology for the acts he had committed. The Iowa court ruled in favor of the plaintiff saying that the statutes provided for the dismissal of a pupil "for gross immorality"

---

[12] Lander v. Seaver, 32 Vt 114 (1859).

[13] Murphy v. Board of Directors of Independent Dist. of Marengo, 30 Iowa 429 (1870).

or "for persistent violation of the regulations of the school" and that there was no indication that the pupil in question was guilty of either offense. The court further ruled:

> . . . while we would not interfere with the action of the board within the range of their jurisdiction and legal discretion, we cannot sanction an exercise of authority not conferred by statute, or the enforcement of penalties, essentially *ex post facto,* under the guise of sound discretion. When proper regulations for the government of the school are made and brought to the knowledge of the pupils, they may well be held to the penalties for their violation; but for the board to visit the severest penalty within their power upon a pupil for an act out of school, not prohibited either expressly or by implication, even by a general regulation, is at variance with both the letter and spirit of our laws.

When a proper hearing is not held as required by law, the exclusion of a pupil from school will not be upheld by the courts.[14] A pupil wrote an article which was published in his father's newspaper and which criticized the management of the school which he attended. The boy was expelled from school upon the allegation that he had attempted to have others write similar articles and that he had urged others to read the articles that were published. The statutes in Massachusetts provided that no child could be excluded permanently from public school without being given the opportunity of being heard. In a hearing requested by Morrison, the father of the boy, the principal of the school supplemented his detailed statement with testimony from teachers saying the boy's actions had had a detrimental effect upon the school. The school committee refused to permit the Morrison boy to call pupils to testify in his behalf on the grounds that such testimony might weaken the authority of the principal and bring discredit upon the school. When the committee was advised that the pupil witnesses were the only testimony that the boy could present in his behalf, the committee modified its

---

[14] Morrison v. Lawrence, 186 Mass 456, 72 NE 91 (1904).

statement by permitting volunteers to testify. No one volunteered, and the pupil was expelled.

The Supreme Judicial Court of Massachusetts said:

How far an administrative board clothed with quasi judicial powers, which has decided upon a definite course of action in a case, will be willing to review its decision, must depend largely upon the sound judgment and sense of justice of its members; but in granting this right to a pupil whom they propose to permanently exclude from the benefit of the public schools, the law presumes that when called upon to reconsider their purpose they will listen patiently to his case as fully as he wishes to present it, so long as such presentation does not range beyond the legitimate limits of the issue involved. When it appears that a fair trial has been given, and the pupil allowed to present the merits of his case, mere errors committed in the admission or exclusion of evidence are not enough to make a final adverse decision.

A member of the senior class of a high school wrote a poem, a satire of the school rules, and directed some younger pupils to take it to the office of the local newspaper which was published weekly. When the poem was published, the children who delivered it were asked by the school authorities to make a "suitable" apology. The principal of the high school suspended the two children when they refused to apologize as requested. The Supreme Court of Wisconsin sustained the action of the principal although no specific rule existed to support his position, and Justice Bashford delivering the opinion of the court stated:

We are not called upon to approve the practical wisdom displayed by the school authorities in dealing with the hasty conduct of thoughtless school children, prompted by an older mate, and abetted by the publisher of the paper, or to justify the strong resentment that must have prompted the relator in appealing to the courts for redress.

The exercise of a little charity, forbearance, and good nature might have avoided the controversy. . . .

* * *

The school authorities considered the misconduct for which the pupils were suspended such as to have a direct and injurious effect upon the good order and discipline of the school. The relator's children were instrumental in causing the publication of the poem in a newspaper, which, supposedly, found its way into the homes of many of the children attending the high school, and who would be as much influenced thereby as if the writing had been printed and posted in the schoolroom, or there circulated and read. The teachers are especially familiar with the disposition and temper of the children under their charge, and the effect which such a publication would probably have upon the good order and discipline of the school. The school authorities must necessarily be invested with a broad discretion in the government and discipline of the pupils, and the courts should not interfere with the exercise of such authority unless it has been illegally or unreasonably exercised. The trial court has found that the act complained of does not evince an abuse of discretion on the part of the teacher, but rather an earnest desire to counsel, admonish, and discipline the pupils for their own good as well as for the good of the school. That conclusion is supported by the testimony and is here approved.[15]

The court in *Wooster* v. *Sunderland* was asked to review the circumstances related to the expulsion of a pupil who had addressed the student body for the purpose of making certain charges against the management of the school.[16] Earl Wooster, a pupil in the high school, openly criticized the management of the school and school property in a meeting of the student body being held in the school auditorium. When the board of education asked Wooster to explain his action, the boy in his explanation admitted

---

[15] State ex rel. Dresser v. District Board of School Dist. No. 1, 135 Wis 619, 116 NW 232 (1908).

[16] Wooster v. Sunderland, 27 CalApp 51, 148 Pac 959 (1915).

that the address was "intended as a slam" at the board. Convinced that Wooster had tried to discredit and humiliate them in front of the student body, the school board demanded an apology and a public retraction of the statements that had been made. The boy refused to comply with the request of the school board and was expelled. The California court pointed out that since the purpose of the address was to belittle the board, to produce disrespect for the board, and to encourage hostility toward the board, the conduct must be classified as insubordination and that the board was within its power to expel the pupil in order to maintain the discipline of the school.

The court held:

In the present case an apology would have been adequate punishment for the misconduct of the plaintiff, and doubtless would have served to prevent a repetition thereof; and at the same time would have tended to correct the evil resulting therefrom. The refusal of the plaintiff to make an apology demanded not only accentuated his misconduct, but made it necessary for the defendants to resort to an order of expulsion as the only effective means of punishing the plaintiff and maintaining the discipline of the school.

§ 6.4 Authority of school officials to require pupils to remain on the school grounds during school hours

"The principle is well established that a board of education may suspend or expel from school any pupil who disobeys a reasonable rule of the board. The rule, however, must be reasonable and it must be within the jurisdiction of the board to make."[17] Courts throughout the country have been petitioned to pass upon the reasonableness and legality of rules which boards of education have adopted in exercising their responsibility and duty to control the pupils in the public schools. Perhaps because school authorities feel that their responsibility for the safety, health, and

---

[17] Newton Edwards, The Courts and The Public Schools (Chicago: The University of Chicago Press, 1955), p. 601.

discipline of pupils may best be fulfilled by providing supervision of their activities throughout the school day, perhaps because local merchants and residents request that pupils not be permitted to leave school without supervision, or perhaps because parents recommend that their children remain at school until the school day is ended, school boards have enacted rules and regulations which require pupils to remain on the school grounds during the prescribed hours for school attendance.   Some pupils who wish to run errands for their parents, who wish to have lunch elsewhere, or who want "to get away" from school for awhile bring pressure to bear upon those enforcing the rules to release them during recess or the lunch hour.   When the rules directly interfere with the plans of parents, often the question is raised concerning the power of schools to exercise a control which overrides the prerogative of parents.

When a parent arranged for her daughter to be given private music instruction by a teacher not employed by the school district, she was told by the school authorities that the child could not be permitted to leave the school grounds during school hours.   The mother was unable to understand the reasoning of the school board and refused to have her daughter comply with the rule.   When the child left the school ground for music lessons as she was instructed to do by her mother, the superintendent suspended her for violating the rule and leaving campus without permission.   The mother appealed to the court for a writ to reinstate her daughter in the public schools, but the Supreme Court of Alabama affirmed the judgment of a lower court in sustaining the rule adopted by the board of education.[18]   The court reasoned:

That the rule adopted by the board was well within their power and discretion is not questioned.   In view of this broad discretion vested in the board, this court can only interfere in the event of an arbitrary exercise or abuse thereof.   Very clearly such a case is not here presented.   The fact that inconvenience, or even some hardship, may result to petitioner and others who desire

---

18 Christian v. Jones, 211 Ala 161, 100 So 99 (1924).

to patronize a music teacher outside the school is but a mere incident, and does not of itself argue the unreasonableness of the rule, abuse of discretion of the board. As a matter of precedent it may be easily seen that to permit what petitioner here seeks might in the course of time prove detrimental to the orderly conduct of the school. In any event, the board has so determined, and no abuse of their discretion appears, and respondent, as superintendent, was but carrying into effect the regulations of the board in suspending petitioner's child.

Some parents in Virginia attacked the validity of a rule prohibiting pupils from leaving campus unaccompanied by a teacher between the hours of 9 a.m. and 3:35 p.m. as being "an unreasonable regulation in restraint of their liberty and the liberty of their children" and as being "an infringement upon their right of property in the school."[19] The facts of the case were that the parents wanted their two children to be excused from the regulation to eat their noon meal at home or at a downtown hotel with the father and the principal refused to grant the special privilege. The children left the campus to have their lunch with their father, and upon returning to school they were suspended for violating the aforesaid regulation. Although it was the contention of the parents that it was their right to provide and select food for their children and to designate where it would be eaten, the Supreme Court of Appeals of Virginia reversed the decision of a lower court and declared the rule reasonable and within the jurisdiction of the school board in conducting the affairs of the school. The court emphasized that it was not passing upon the wisdom or "unwisdom" of enacting the rule but that its concern was with the reasonableness of the regulation.

The court noted that no one had a vested property right in the public schools and that:

While it may be a restraint upon liberty and an infringement upon happiness for the Legislature to inhibit a parent from sending his child to any school, it is neither

---

[19] Flory v. Smith, 145 Va 164, 134 SE 360 (1926).

restraint nor infringement for the Legislature to enact laws to debar a child from the mere privilege of acquiring an education at the expense of the state until he is willing to submit himself to all reasonable regulations enacted for the purpose of promoting efficiency and maintaining discipline.

Other courts called upon to pass upon the reasonableness of school board rules requiring pupils to remain on campus during the school lunch period have ruled similarly.[20] A Texas court saw nothing unreasonable, harsh or oppressive in such a rule and said there was no question of a board's power to enact a rule which was designed to protect the health of the pupils committed to its care.[21] Although confinement of pupils to the school grounds may have a detrimental effect upon business operation of nearby merchants, it is of no consequence when the rule is enacted in good faith and for the welfare of the pupils.[22] Representative of the reasoning of the court in upholding the authority of school boards to adopt such resolutions is the statement made by the Supreme Court of Nebraska:

> During school hours . . . general education and the control of pupils who attend public schools are in the hands of school boards, superintendents, principals and teachers. This control extends to health, proper surroundings, necessary discipline, promotion of morality and other wholesome influences, while parental authority is temporarily superseded. Cafeterias are recognized adjuncts to public high schools. Some pupils come long distances and cannot return to their homes for noon

---

20 Bishop v. Houston Independent School Dist., 119 Tex 403, 29 SW (2d) 312 (1930); Bishop v. Houston Independent School District, 35 SW(2d) 465 (Texas, 1931); Richardson v. Braham, 125 Neb 142, 249 NW 557 (1933); Haffner v. Braham, 125 Neb 147, 249 NW 560 (1933); Casey County Board of Education v. Luster, 282 SW(2d) 333 (Ky., 1955).

21 Bishop v. Houston Independent School Dist., 119 Tex 403, 29 SW(2d) 312 (1930).

22 Bozeman v. Morrow, 34 SW(2d) 654 (Texas, 1931); Richardson v. Braham, 125 Neb 142, 249 NW 557 (1933); Haffner v. Braham, 125 Neb 147, 249 NW 560 (1933); Casey County Board of Education v. Luster, 282 SW(2d) 333 (Ky., 1955).

meals. Resort of pupils to public eating places in business districts of a city beyond both parental care and the control of teachers may mar the work and defeat to some extent the purposes of public education.[23]

Not only have the courts upheld rules of a general nature which restrict pupils to school grounds during school hours, but in the case of *Casey County Board of Education* v. *Luster* the Court of Civil Appeals of Kentucky held reasonable a rule which a principal made declaring "no one, while in school, shall be allowed to enter the restaurant of Mr. Russell or any other business establishment in the town without permission from 8:15 a.m. until 3:00 p.m."[24] The specified cafe was adjoining the school grounds, and pupils could make purchases without leaving the campus. The school insisted that the rule was not adopted to interfere with the business of Mr. Russell or to force pupils to eat in the school lunchroom. The court held:

> It cannot be successfully contended that the regulation prohibiting the children from entering or patronizing the Russell cafe during school hours was unreasonable and arbitrary. It is common knowledge that children, if allowed to depend upon their own selection, often indulge themselves in unbalanced diets. Furthermore, if uncontrolled at table young children are apt to engage in rough or uncouth practices and conduct. If the school lunch is to be successful then all children who purchase their noon meal may be required to do so from the school lunchroom. The regulation appears to be for the common good of all children attending this school and we find that it is not unreasonable or arbitrary.

In recent years the problems arising from pupils' driving automobiles to school have become more widespread and in some areas have prompted school authorities to adopt rules concerning the operation of the vehicles during school

---

[23] Richardson v. Braham, 125 Neb 142, 249 NW 557 (1933).
[24] Casey County Board of Education v. Luster, 282 SW(2d) 333 (Ky., 1955).

hours. The McLean Independent School District adopted a rule which required pupils to park their automobiles in the school parking lot upon arrival at school and leave them parked until 3:45 p.m. or until special permission was granted to move them. When Marsha Andrews was suspended from school because she persisted in parking her car away from school and driving it home and back during the lunch period as instructed by her father, her father brought action against the school board for the wrongful exclusion of his daughter.[25]   The trial court upheld the contention of Andrews that the girl had been suspended under the provisions of a rule which was void and which was not within the authority of the board to make.   Upon appeal the Court of Civil Appeals of Texas reversed the judgment of the lower court.

Testimony was presented by the president of the school board which showed that the increase in the number of pupils driving their automobiles to school had created a danger for the pupils who were on the high school campus and the adjoining playground for the elementary school children.   The higher court, convinced that the motives for enacting such a rule were for the protection of the children, upheld the school board in its regulation:

> The regulation was not for the purpose of exercising authority over the use of public streets and highways at all . . . but for the purpose of controlling the conduct of the students to the end that student pedestrians on the streets adjacent to the schools might be safe from student operated automobiles and that better order, decorum and discipline might prevail at the noon recess. We do not believe they abused their discretion in so doing.

The court made a suggestion to the school board:

> Since all parties assumed Marsha Andrews "drove her automobile to school" within the purview of the regulation in question we may so assume, but we can anticipate

---

[25] McLean Independent School Dist. v. Andrews, 333 SW(2d) 886 (Texas, 1960).

further complications in the regulation as worded. For example, students might park their automobiles two or more blocks away from school, or in town, walk to them and drive them during the noon recess. Technically they might not be "driving automobiles to school" but would still be guilty of the principal acts the school authorities testified the regulation was passed to prohibit, viz., driving their automobiles at the noon recess. We would respectfully suggest that the purpose sought to be accomplished might be more specifically stated by the following rule, or one of similar language: "School children shall not be permitted to drive automobiles during the lunch period nor anytime after they arrive at school each day until they leave at ―――― p.m. (the time the school is dismissed for the day), unless by special permission of the school authorities."

§ 6.5 Summary

School personnel in daily contact with large numbers of children find it necessary to place certain restrictions upon the personal freedom of pupils if they are to provide the maximum educational opportunities for boys and girls and if they are to fulfill their responsibilities to the community and the state. Realizing the necessity for orderly conduct and good discipline in the schools, the legislatures of the many states have seen fit to clothe boards of education with broad discretionary powers in the management and control of pupil personnel. The courts express a reluctance to interfere with the operation of the school except where a clear abuse of this discretionary power is evident; but if school authorities exceed the limits of their jurisdiction or employ measures which are deemed unreasonable, oppressive, or arbitrary, the courts will not hesitate to declare such actions or rules void and against the best interest of the schools and the public. Since the ultimate boundaries for the extent of control that school authorities may exercise in the administration of pupil personnel are drawn by the courts, a consideration of the judicial decisions relating to damage to school property, public ridicule or criticism of the school, and confinement to the school grounds during school hours will aid in establishing a set of legal principles regarding the legal limitations and obligations of school authorities in these areas of pupil control.

The cost of replacing damaged or destroyed property of the school is reported to have increased steadily during the past few years. To defray the expense incurred by accidental, willful, or malicious damage to school property by pupils, school boards have passed rules and regulations which require pupils to pay for the damage they inflict; and at least half of the state legislatures, responding to public request, have enacted parent responsibility laws. Since the first case came before a high court in 1880, courts have been called upon in several instances to consider cases arising from the enforcement of these rules, regulations, and laws.

The courts have been of one accord in ruling that a school board rule is unreasonable that provides for the suspension or expulsion of a child for nonpayment of damages to school property which he accidentally broke or destroyed. The Supreme Court of Iowa in *Perkins* v. *Board of Directors of the Independent School Dist. of West Des Moines, supra,* §6.2, n 6, declared it beyond the authority of school directors to expel a pupil from public school for his refusal to pay for a window of the schoolhouse which he broke accidently and "without intention of wrong." Emphasizing that carelessness is a common fault of children, the Supreme Court of Indiana in *State* v. *Vanderbilt, supra,* § 6.2, n 7, declared the school board rule which required pupils to "pay for the wanton and careless destruction of school property" unreasonable and added that a teacher who tried to enforce such a rule through the use of corporal punishment could be found guilty of assault and battery. In Michigan, *Holman* v. *School Trustees of Avon, supra,* § 6.2, n 8, a father appealed to the courts to reinstate in the public school his child who had been excluded for refusal to pay one dollar for a windowpane accidently broken. The Michigan court refused to uphold the rule of the school directors under which the boy was expelled and pointed out that some children could be denied the opportunity of an education for their inability to pay for a careless or negligent act.

Three cases have been reported which deal with the validity of statutes holding parents liable for the actions of their child who damages school property willfully or maliciously. The Supreme Court of South Dakota in *Lamro Independent Consol. School Dist. No. 20 of Tripp County* v. *Cawthorne, supra,* § 6.2, n 9, dismissed the petition of a school board which sought to recover damages from the parents of a boy who intentionally injured school property. Since the act was committed outside of school hours and not in the presence of a teacher, the court reasoned that the statute which held parents responsible for the damage of school property "on the complaint of the teacher" was not applicable.

Four years later in the case of *Board of Education of Palmyra* v. *Hansen, supra,* § 6.2, n 10, a New Jersey court rendered a judgment in favor of the school board that sought to recover damages in the amount of $344,000 from the parents of a boy who purposely set fire to a school building. The court reasoned that when one avails himself of the benefits of public school, he automatically subjects himself to the statutes which apply to the public schools. When a child set fire "maliciously and willfully" to the school draperies an insurance company brought suit against the parents to recover damages allowed under the state law. The Supreme Court of North Carolina in the case of *General Ins. Co. of America* v. *Faulkner, supra,* § 6.2, n 11, told the parents that although the property damage was covered by insurance, the parents remained liable for the amount of damages as specified by statute.

The authority of school officials to punish pupils who publicly criticize or ridicule the school has been challenged by those who feel that a control of this type is an interference with personal liberties guaranteed them by the constitutions of the state and the nation. A Vermont court did not uphold the contention of the plaintiff who insisted that the teacher had no authority to punish his child for an act committed out of school hours and away from school.

The reasoning of the court in *Lander* v. *Seaver, supra,* § 6.3, n 12, was that since the boy had ridiculed the teacher in the presence of other pupils, his action had ". . . a direct and immediate tendency to injure the school, to subvert the master's authority, and to beget disorder and insubordination." An Iowa court in *Murphy* v. *Board of Directors of Independent Dist. of Marengo, supra,* § 6.3, n 13, ruled to the contrary when a father brought action against the school board for the wrongful exclusion of his son who had written articles ridiculing the school board. Since the statutes of the state provided for dismissal of a pupil only upon the grounds of "gross immorality" or "persistent violation of the regulations of the school," the court refused to support the school board in its action.

The court in *Morrison* v. *Lawrence, supra,* § 6.3, n 14, emphasized the importance of conducting a proper hearing before excluding permanently from the schools a boy who wrote articles which tended to have a detrimental effect upon the discipline of the school. Another instance concerning the exclusion of pupils from school because of their publications may be found in *State ex rel. Dresser* v. *District Board of School Dist. No. 1, supra,* § 6.3, n 15. Two children who refused to apologize for submitting for publication a poem which was a "take-off" on school rules were suspended from school. The Supreme Court of Wisconsin sustained the school board in its suspension saying that teachers were in a position to know what was detrimental to the best interests of the school.

In the case of *Wooster* v. *Sunderland, supra,* § 6.3, n 16, a California court upheld the expulsion of a boy from school who made an address to the student body designed to humiliate and bring disrespect to the school board. The court classified his conduct as insubordination and declared it within the power of the school board to exclude the pupil in order to maintain the discipline of the school.

When pupils arrive at school, they necessarily come under the control and supervision of school authorities. The courts have consistently upheld the rules adopted by school boards which help the schools fulfill their responsibilities to the pupils, parents, and community by requiring pupils to remain on the school grounds during school hours. An Alabama court in *Christian* v. *Jones, supra,* § 6.4, n 18, ruled that it was within the power of school authorities to refuse permission to a child to leave the school grounds for special music instruction arranged by her mother. When parents in Virginia caused their children to violate a school rule prohibiting them from leaving school unaccompanied by a teacher by taking them to lunch at a downtown hotel, the children were suspended from school. Although the parent denounced the school rule as being an interference with his liberty and the liberty of his children, the court in *Flory* v. *Smith, supra,* § 6.4, n 19, declared the rule reasonable and within the power of the school board to adopt. Other courts called upon to pass upon the reasonableness of school board rules requiring pupils to remain on campus during the lunch period have ruled similarly. One court, *Bishop* v. *Houston Independent School Dist., supra,* § 6.4, nn 20, and 21, recognized such a rule as being designed to protect the health of pupils. Another court in *Richardson* v. *Braham, supra,* § 6.4, nn 20 and 23, proclaimed the reasonableness of such a rule on the grounds that adult supervision was necessary for children during the lunch period. Although requiring pupils to remain on the school grounds may have a detrimental effect upon nearby businesses, it is of little consideration when the rule is enacted in good faith and for the welfare of the pupils.

The Court of Civil Appeals of Texas upheld a school rule which provided that pupils who drove their automobiles to school must park them upon arrival and leave them parked until the end of the school day. In making the decision in *McLean Independent School Dist.* v. *Andrews, supra,* § 6.4, n 25, the court relied heavily upon testimony presented to show that the rule was enacted for the protection of pupils who might be playing or walking in the vicinity in which the automobiles were being operated.

In the operation of the public schools boards of education, administrators, and teachers are called upon often to make decisions which necessarily entail the use of discretion. The instances of litigation reported in this chapter dealing with the limitations, obligations, and responsibilities of school authorities in the control of certain types of willful misconduct reemphasize the limits to which the courts will go to uphold school authorities in the operation, management, and control of the public schools.

Chapter 7

CONCLUSIONS AND RECOMMENDATIONS

Section
7.1   Conclusions
7.2   Recommendations

§ 7.1 Conclusions

In each of the fifty states may be found constitutional provisions for educating the youth of the state, but attendance in the public schools is not a guaranteed right to be exercised exclusive of all other considerations; rather, it is a privilege which may be claimed by those young people who are willing to comply with the provisions of the constitution and statutes of the state and to submit to such reasonable rules and regulations as the local school authorities may adopt. The power of school authorities to control the pupils within their charge is for the most part derived from their discretionary grant of power which gives them the right and authority to make and enforce reasonable rules and regulations for the good government, good order, and efficient operation of the schools and is limited only by constitutional provisions, legislative enactments, and judicial interpretation of the law.

Confronted by the daily problems involved in the operation and management of the public schools, school boards given the general superintendence and control of public schools by the legislatures of the states have found it necessary to adopt policies and enact rules and regulations in dealing with pupil personnel which may require individuals to relinquish to some degree their personal freedom for the welfare of others and the general well-being of the school. Lacking specific statutes to guide their actions, school boards attempting to discharge their duty often enact rules which are challenged as being unreasonable, oppressive, arbitrary, or illegal. When individuals feel that the school board has infringed upon their rights, has adopted rules that are unreasonable under the existing circumstances, or has exceeded the authority granted it by

162

the legislature, they sometimes express hostility to the rules. Extreme instances of disagreement have resulted in court cases not confined to any particular area of the United States; but for each case litigated, many controversies arise which never reach the courts because it is easier and less expensive to submit to the restrictions than to litigation, because the question involved becomes moot, or because the issue is resolved satisfactorily on a local level.

When the various judicial bodies are called upon to adjudicate a disagreement, they express a reluctance to interfere with the operation and management of the schools by local school authorities unless there is a clear abuse of authority. As anxious as the courts may seem to be to uphold the school authorities in the exercise of their duty, there is no doubt that they will declare void and unreasonable a rule which is not enacted in good faith, which is unreasonable, and which is contrary to legislative and constitutional provisions. In making disposition of a case, the courts throughout the country give judicial cognizance to the opinions of other courts in their jurisdiction and other jurisdictions in similar cases. The courts do not pass upon the wisdom or expediency of the rule in question, but the circumstances peculiar to each case are reviewed in the light of the authority of the school officials to enact the rule, the constitutionality of the rule, and the reasonableness of the action taken by the school authorities.

An examination of the instances of litigation relating to pupil control may reveal certain legal principles which may serve as a legal framework for the actions of school boards and administrators who deal daily with a multiplicity of problems in the administration of pupil personnel. The decisions of the courts presented in this study may be summarized in the following legal principles:

1. The courts will uphold the action of school boards in attempting to maintain and promote good order and discipline in the public schools unless there is a clear abuse of authority.

2. When school authorities exclude pupils from the public schools for violating reasonable rules and regulations,

the courts will sanction the action only as it conforms to the constitutional and statutory provisions for exclusion of pupils from the schools.

3. Although secret societies meet away from school and out of school hours, boards of education are within their authority to enforce statutes permitting or requiring suspension and/or expulsion from the public schools of pupils who hold membership in secret societies considered by school authorities to be detrimental to the best interest of the school.

4. In the presence of supportive legislation, boards of education may deny credit and withhold the diploma from any pupil who violates an antifraternity statute.

5. In the absence of specific statutory authority, if evidence can be presented to show that membership in secret societies is detrimental to the discipline and good order of the school, school authorities may limit the participation of fraternity and sorority members in activities of the school to classroom instruction.

6. When secret societies may be proved to have an ill effect upon the discipline and welfare of the schools and when contrary legislation does not exist, school authorities may deny participation in extracurricular activities to any pupil who refuses to sign a pledge stating that he is not a member of such a society.

7. Rules and regulations adopted by school boards which prohibit membership in secret societies during summer vacation periods may not be upheld by the courts and may be considered an invasion of parental authority.

8. Pupils who marry are not amenable to the compulsory school law.

9. Pupils may not be excluded legally from school on the sole basis of marital status.

10. Some doubt remains that school boards may legally limit participation of pupils in any school activity solely on the basis of marital status.

11. An earnest attempt to protect the health of a pregnant pupil and concern for the welfare of the student

body may justify the suspension of the pupil from school during the period of her pregnancy.

12. Local school authorities may deny participation in graduation exercises to a pupil who refuses to wear a cap and gown.

13. A school board rule which provides for withholding grades and a diploma from a pupil who refuses to wear a cap and gown for the graduation ceremony is unreasonable.

14. That school authorities may prescribe the type of dress to be worn by pupils of the public school is doubtful.

15. School authorities may prohibit unconventional clothes or personal appearance which has an adverse effect upon the discipline of the school or which damages school property beyond normal wear.

16. When the school population or community is threatened with an epidemic of smallpox, the legislature, board of health, or school board may make vaccination a condition of school attendance.

17. When the statute providing for vaccination of children who attend the public school is mandatory, school boards must enforce the regulation.

18. School boards must subordinate their authority to the authority of health departments when there is an immediate threat to the health of the community.

19. School authorities may exclude from the public schools any child who is so seriously handicapped physically or mentally as to impede the progress of other pupils, disrupt classroom discipline, and present an undue number of problems for the teacher.

20. Parents may be found in violation of the compulsory school attendance law if they refuse to permit their child to attend the special school for physically or mentally handicapped children to which he has been assigned by the school authorities.

21. School boards are within their authority to exclude from school children who pose a threat to the health of other children.

22. Rules requiring physical examination of all pupils each school year may be upheld by the courts if sufficient evidence is produced to show that the examination is required to prevent the spread of disease and to furnish necessary health information to the teachers.

23. A rule of the board of education which requires pupils to pay for carelessly inflicted damages to school property is unreasonable.

24. When parent responsibility statutes are present, school boards may be able to hold parents liable for damages which their child does to school property willfully and maliciously.

25. School authorities may punish a pupil who publicly criticizes or ridicules the school if his actions may be proved to have an ill effect upon the discipline of the school.

26. School officials may enact rules and regulations which require pupils to remain on the school grounds during school hours.

§ 7.2 Recommendations

The discussion of court cases throughout this book has been of an objective nature. Legal principles derived from the judicial decisions are listed above. The following suggestions or recommendations are somewhat subjective and may not be agreed upon by all. Nevertheless, it is contended that they are based upon firm legal principles as well as on principles of sound school administration.

1. Formulate policies of pupil control within framework of the law. All rules and regulations purported to control pupil behavior in the public school should be in conformity with constitutional and statutory provisions. Dissatisfaction with the existing laws is no valid ground for the violation thereof. The law should be obeyed. The remedy for objectionable laws is to seek their repeal or amendment.

2. Seek legal advice when in doubt of the law. In the absence or vagueness of a law regarding a school rule or regulation which is disputed, teachers, as well as other concerned parties, should seek the advice of someone who,

by virtue of training and experience, is professionally qualified to render reliable advice as to legal and proper action.
An attorney general, a state superintendent of education, a
lawyer, a professor of law, or a professor of school administration may sometimes be helpful.   The person who has
a background in both law and school administration is most
ideally equipped to render legal advice on matters of pupil
control or any other aspects of the public schools.

**3. Establish no rule or method of enforcement which
is unnecessary.**   No rule or regulation for pupil conduct
should be formulated nor no method of enforcement
employed which is not contributory and necessary for the
benefit and welfare of the pupil and the school.   Rules
and regulations which are not purposeful cannot be justified.

**4. Establish positive approach in curbing secret
societies.**   There is little need for written rules and regulations prohibiting secret societies without evidence of their
existence and harm.   Where they do exist and operate in
such a manner as to seriously undermine school morale
they should be dealt with sternly even to the point of
temporarily excluding members from school until there
is evidence that their affiliation is terminated.   Even
though the legality of school board policies of prohibiting
these organizations by such punitive measures is now firmly
established by judicial opinion, a more positive approach
on a long time basis would be to substitute attractive school
activities which would obviate the pupils' demand for
fraternities and sororities.

**5. Do not discriminate against married high-school
pupils.**   School boards should exercise extreme caution in
adopting policies designed to penalize all pupils who marry.
There is growing doubt in the judiciary and elsewhere as
to the legality and propriety of school boards to attempt to
curtail high-school marriages by discriminatory, punitive,
or other means. Determination of the minimum age
limits for marriages is a sociological problem to be dealt
with by the legislature and not the school board. Of course
the school board should have the authority to adopt rules
as are necessary for the proper conduct of the school.

School officials always have had—and likely always will have—judicial sanction in prohibiting pupils from school attendance or barring them from participation in certain school activities, when it is evident that their attendance or participation is injurious to the morale and the conduct of the school. It should be emphasized, however, that this applies to all pupils regardless of marital status.

6. **Minimize rules regulating the dress of pupils.** Pupils should not be compelled to wear "strait jackets." Prudence should be exercised in dealing with pupils whose dress varies from the norm. Publicized regulations regarding the matter could, by suggestion, motivate some pupils to dress in such peculiar fashion as to draw attention. Usually the fads in pupil attire fade when ignored by teachers and others. Disturbing extremes in individual cases can usually be controlled better by personal counseling with the pupil or the parent rather than by publicized and senational measures which could lead to animosity and litigation.

7. **Consider carefully the school's legal responsibilities and legal limitations in health measures.** School officials and teachers should be guided by competent health authorities as to what responsibilities, within legal limitations, should be assumed by the school for the maintenance and protection of the pupils' health. An instructional program in the school for developing good health would always be legal and should be emphasized. Examination of the pupils' physical conditions is usually proper and legal; administering treatment for physical disorders is more likely to encounter parental and legal opposition. School personnel would do well to consider carefully their legal liabilities for pupil injuries from improper and unauthorized treatment of pupils.

8. **Use punitive measures only as a last resort in combating willful misbehavior.** School personnel should draw upon their own professional resources before forcing into the courts the settlement of cases growing out of pupil misconduct. Usually a cause may be found for the misbehavior of a pupil. Punishment for the improper conduct

does not remove the cause of the act. Despite the judicial sanction of punitive measures for misconduct, such as corporal punishment, suspension, or expulsion, they should be employed as a last resort. More defensible deterrents of misbehavior are a challenging curriculum, an adequate guidance program, and effective teaching. None of these would lead to litigation and unwholesome public relations.

9. Apply legal principles to improve school and community relations. Finally, it is recommended that legal principles pertaining to pupil control be applied judiciously in the educational and administrative processes. Perhaps the most important consideration in the application of a legal principle is the probable effect on the school and community. The fact that an act is legal is no assurance that it is necessary or desirable. It may be performed in complete accord with a permissive law and be sanctioned by judicial opinion, but, if it results in community resentment and dissatisfaction, it might better not have been performed at all. Legal principles are best applied when school conduct is in accord with the laws, but they should also be applied in a manner which will serve the welfare of the pupil, school, and community.

TABLE OF CASES

References are to sections.

Calway v. Williamson, 130 Conn 575, 36 A(2d) 377 (1944), 1.2

Carr v. Inhabitants of Dighton, 229 Mass 304, 118 NE 525 (1918), 5.4, 5.5

Carson, Commonwealth ex rel. v. Rowe, 218 Pa 168, 67 Atl 56 (1907), 5.2

Casey County Board of Education v. Luster (Ky), 282 SW(2d) 333 (1955), 6.4

Christian v. Jones, 211 Ala 161, 100 So 99 (1924), 6.4, 6.5

City of New Braunfels v. Waldschmidt, 109 Tex 302, 207 SW 303 (1918), reversing judgment Waldschmidt v. New Braunfels, 193 SW 1077, 5.2

Cochrane v. Board of Education of Mesick Consolidated School Dist., 360 Mich 390, 103 NW(2d) 569 (1960), 3.4, 3.5

Coggin v. Board of Education of Durham, 223 NC 763, 28 SE(2d) 527 (1944), 2.3, 2.4

Commonwealth v. Aiken, 64 PaSuperCt 96 (1916), 5.2

Commonwealth v. Butler, 76 PaSuperCt 113 (1920), 5.2

Commonwealth v. Childs, 299 Mass 367, 12 NE(2d) 814 (1938), 5.2

Commonwealth v. Green, 268 Mass 585, 168 NE 101 (1929), 5.2

Commonwealth v. Smith, 9 PaDistRep 625 (1900), 5.2

Commonwealth v. Wilkins, 75 PaSuperCt 305 (1920), 5.2

Commonwealth ex rel. Carson v. Rowe, 218 Pa 168, 67 Atl 56 (1907), 5.2

Commonwealth ex rel. Schaffer v. Wilkins, 271 Pa 523, 115 Atl 887 (1922), 5.2

Connell v. Gray, 33 Okla 591, 127 Pac 417 (1912), 4.2, 4.4

Cox, State ex rel. v. Board of Education of Salt Lake City, 21 Utah 401, 60 Pac 1013 (1900), 5.2

Cram v. School Board of Manchester, 82 NH 495, 136 Atl 263 (1927), 5.2

Crane v. School Dist. No. 14 of Tillamook County, 95 Ore 644, 188 Pac 712 (1920), 5.4, 5.5

Dresser, State ex rel. v. District Board of School Dist. No. 1, 135 Wis 619, 116 NW 232 (1908), 6.3, 6.5

Duffield v. School Dist. of Williamsport, 162 Pa 476, 29 Atl 742 (1894), 5.2

Dunham v. Board of Education of City School Dist. of Cincinnati (Ohio), 98 NE(2d) 594 (1950), 5.2

Dunham, State ex rel. v. Board of Education of City School Dist. of Cincinnati, 154 OhioSt 469, 96 NE(2d) 413 (1951), 5.2, 5.5

Exposito v. Barber, 74 NJSuper 289, 181 A(2d) 201 (1962), 5.4, 5.5

Favorite v. Board of Education of Chicago, 235 Ill 314, 84 NE 402 (1908), 2.3, 2.4

Field v. Robinson, 198 Pa 638, 48 Atl 873 (1901), 5.2

Flory v. Smith, 145 Va 164, 134 SE 360 (1926), 6.4, 6.5

Freeman, State ex rel. v. Zimmerman, 86 Minn 353, 90 NW 783 (1902), 5.2

McFadden, State ex rel. v. Shorrock, 55 Wash 208, 104 Pac 214 (1909), 5.2

McLean Independent School Dist. v. Andrews (Tex), 333 SW(2d) 886 (1960), 6.4, 6.5

McLeod v. State ex rel. Colmer, 154 Miss 468, 122 So 737 (1929), 3.3, 3.5

McSween v. Board of School Trustees of Ft. Worth, 60 TexCivApp 270, 129 SW 206 (1910), 5.2

March, In re, 140 PaSuper 472, 14 A(2d) 368 (1940), 5.2

Marsh v. Earle (Pa), 24 FSupp 385 (1938), 5.2

Martin v. Craig, 42 ND 213, 173 NW 787 (1919), 5.4, 5.5

Matheson v. Brady, 202 Ga 500, 43 SE(2d) 703 (1947), 4.3, 4.4

Mathews v. Board of Education of School Dist. No. 1 of Kalamazoo, 127 Mich 530, 86 NW 1036 (1901), 5.2

Metcalf v. State, 21 TexApp 174, 17 SW 142 (1886), 1.2

Milhoof, State ex rel. v. Board of Education of Barberton, 76 OhioSt 297, 81 NE 568 (1907), 5.2

Mitchell v. McCall, 273 Ala 604, 143 S(2d) 629 (1962), 4.2, 4.4

Morrison v. Lawrence, 186 Mass 456, 72 NE 91 (1904), 6.3, 6.5

Mosier v. Barren County Board of Health, 308 Ky 829, 215 SW(2d) 967 (1948), 5.2

Murphy v. Board of Directors of Independent Dist. of Marengo, 30 Iowa 429 (1870), 6.3, 6.5

New Braunfels v. Waldschmidt, 109 Tex 302, 207 SW 303 (1918), reversing judgment Waldschmidt v. New Braunfels, 193 SW 1077, 5.2

Nutt v. Board of Education of Goodland, Sherman County, 128 Kan 507, 278 Pac 1065 (1929), 3.3, 3.5

O'Bannon, State ex rel. v. Cole, 220 Mo 697, 119 SW 424 (1909), 5.2

Osborn v. Russell, 64 Kan 507, 68 Pac 60 (1902), 5.2

People v. Ekerold, 211 NY 386, 105 NE 670 (1914), 5.2

People v. McIlwain, 151 NYS 366 (1915), 5.2

People ex rel. Hill v. Board of Education of Lansing, 224 Mich 388, 195 NW 95 (1923), 5.2

People ex rel. Jenkins v. Board of Education of Chicago, 234 Ill 422, 84 NE 1046 (1908), 5.2

People ex rel. La Baugh v. Board of Education of Dist. No. 2, 177 Ill 572, 52 NE 850 (1899), 5.2

People ex rel. Lamme v. Buckland, 84 Colo 240, 269 Pac 15 (1928), 4.2, 4.4

People of State of Illinois ex rel. Pratt v. Wheaton Col., 40 Ill 186 (1866), 2.3, 2.4

Perkins v. Board of Directors of Independent School Dist. of West Des Moines, 56 Iowa 476, 9 NW 356 (1880), 6.2, 6.5

Pierce v. Board of Education of Fulton, 219 NYS(2d) 519 (1961), 5.2

Potts v. Breen, 167 Ill 67, 47 NE 81 (1897), 5.2

State ex rel. Dunham v. Board of Education of City School Dist. of Cincinnati, 154 OhioSt 469, 96 NE(2d) 413 (1951), 5.2, 5.5

State ex rel. Freeman v. Zimmerman, 86 Minn 353, 90 NW 783 (1902), 5.2

State ex rel. Horne v. Biel, 157 Ind 25, 60 NE 672 (1901), 5.2

State ex rel. Lehman v. Partlow, 119 Wash 316, 205 Pac 420 (1922), 5.2

State ex rel. McFadden v. Shorrock, 55 Wash 208, 104 Pac 214 (1909), 5.2

State ex rel. Milhoof v. Board of Education of Barberton, 76 OhioSt 297, 81 NE 568 (1907), 5.2

State ex rel. O'Bannon v. Cole, 220 Mo 697, 119 SW 424 (1909), 5.2

State ex rel. Stallard v. White, 82 Ind 278 (1882), 2.3, 2.4

State in Interest of Goodwin, In re, 214 La 1062, 39 S(2d) 731 (1949), 3.2, 3.5

State of Iowa v. Ghrist, 222 Iowa 1069, 272 NW 440 (1937), 5.3

State of Ohio v. Gans, 168 OhioSt 174, 151 NE(2d) 709 (1958), 3.2, 3.5

State of Ohio v. Turney, 31 OhioCC 222 (1909), 1.2

State of Ohio ex rel. Baker v. Stevenson, 189 NE(2d) 181 (1962), 3.4, 3.5

State of Ohio ex rel. Dunham v. Board of Education of City School Dist. of Cincinnati, 341 US 915, 71 SCt 736 (1951), 5.2

State of Ohio ex rel. Idle v. Chamberlain, 175 NE(2d) 539 (1961), 3.3, 3.5, 5.4, 5.5

State of Tennessee ex rel. Thompson v. Marion County Board of Education, 202 Tenn 29, 302 SW(2d) 57 (1957), 3.3, 3.5

Steele v. Sexton, 253 Mich 32, 234 NW 436 (1931), 2.2, 2.4

Stone v. Probst, 165 Minn 361, 206 NW 642 (1925), 5.4, 5.5

Streich v. Board of Education of Independent School Dist. of Aberdeen, 34 SD 169, 147 NW 779 (1914), 5.4, 5.5

Stromberg v. French, 60 ND 750, 236 NW 477 (1931), 4.3, 4.4

Stull v. Reber, 215 Pa 156, 64 Atl 419 (1906), 5.2

Sutton v. Board of Education of Springfield, 306 Ill 507, 138 NE 131 (1923), 2.2, 2.4

Thompson, State of Tennessee ex rel. v. Marion County Board of Education, 202 Tenn 29, 302 SW(2d) 57 (1957), 3.3, 3.5

Valentine v. Independent School Dist. of Casey, 187 Iowa 555, 174 NW 334 (1919), 4.2, 4.4

Valentine v. Independent School Dist. of Casey, 191 Iowa 1100, 183 NW 434 (1921), 4.2, 4.4

Viemeister v. White, 179 NY 235, 72 NE 97 (1904), 5.2

Vonnegurt v. Baun, 206 Ind 172, 188 NE 677 (1934), 5.2

Walters, In re, 32 NYS 322 (1895), 5.2

Watson v. Cambridge, 157 Mass 561, 32 NE 864 (1893), 5.3, 5.5

Waugh v. Board of Trustees of Univ. of Mississippi (Mississippi), 237 US 589, 35 SCt 720 (1915), 2.2, 2.4

LEGAL BIBLIOGRAPHICAL AIDS

AMERICAN DIGEST SYSTEM. By the Publisher's Editorial
Staff, St. Paul, Minnesota, West Publishing Company.
Including:

CENTURY DIGEST. Vol. 43, 1903. Digest of all reported
cases from 1658 to 1896.

FIRST DECENNIAL DIGEST. Vol. 17, 1910. Digest of all
reported cases from 1897 to 1906.

SECOND DECENNIAL DIGEST. Vol. 20, 1922. Digest of
all reported cases from 1906 to 1916.

THIRD DECENNIAL DIGEST. Vol. 24, 1929. Digest of
all reported cases from 1916 to 1926.

FOURTH DECENNIAL DIGEST. Vol. 27, 1938. Digest of
all reported cases from 1926 to 1936.

FIFTH DECENNIAL DIGEST. Vol. 39, 1949. Digest of
all reported cases from 1936 to 1946.

SIXTH DECENNIAL DIGEST. Vol. 26, 1958. Digest of all
reported cases from 1946 to 1956.

GENERAL DIGEST. Published annually from 1956
to date, with monthly supplements.

AMERICAN JURISPRUDENCE. By the Publisher's Editorial Staff,
Rochester, New York, The Lawyer's Co-operative Publishing Company. Vol. 47, 1943.

AMERICAN LAW REPORTS. By the Publisher's Editorial Staff,
Rochester, New York, The Lawyer's Co-operative Publishing Company. Published annually since 1918.

BLACK'S LAW DICTIONARY. Edited by Henry C. Black.
Fourth Edition. St. Paul: West Publishing Company,
1951.

CORPUS JURIS. Edited by William Mack and others. New
York: The American Law Book Company, Vol. 56, 1932.

CORPUS JURIS SECUNDUM. Edited by Francis J. Ludes and
Harold J. Gilbert. New York: The American Law Book
Company. Vols. 78 and 79, 1952.

NATIONAL REPORTER SYSTEM. St. Paul: West Publishing Company. 1879 and published to date with weekly advance sheets. Including:

THE ATLANTIC REPORTER. Reports in full every decision of the courts of last resort of Connecticut, Delaware, Maryland, New Hampshire, New Jersey, Pennsylvania, Rhode Island, and Vermont from 1885 to date.

THE CALIFORNIA REPORTER. Reports in full every decision of the California Supreme Court and lower courts of record in California from 1959 to date.

THE FEDERAL REPORTER. Reports in full decisions of the United States District Courts and the United States Circuit Courts and other federal courts from 1880 to date.

THE FEDERAL SUPPLEMENT. Reports in full the decisions of the District Courts of the United States since 1932, Court of Claims since 1932 to 1960, and United States Customs Court since 1949 to present.

THE NEW YORK SUPPLEMENT. Reports in full all cases of the New York Court of Appeals and lower courts of record in New York from 1888 to date.

THE NORTH EASTERN REPORTER. Reports in full every decision of the courts of last resort of Illinois, Indiana, Massachusetts, New York, and Ohio from 1885 to date.

THE NORTH WESTERN REPORTER. Reports in full every decision of the courts of last resort in Iowa, Michigan, Minnesota, Nebraska, North Dakota, South Dakota, and Wisconsin from 1879 to date.

THE PACIFIC REPORTER. Reports in full every decision of the courts of last resort of Alaska, Arizona, California, Colorado, Hawaii, Idaho, Kansas, Montana, Nevada, New Mexico, Oklahoma, Oregon, Utah, Washington, and Wyoming from 1883 to date.

THE SOUTH EASTERN REPORTER. Reports in full every decision of the courts of last resort in Georgia,

North Carolina, South Carolina, Virginia, and West Virginia from 1887 to date.

THE SOUTHERN REPORTER. Reports in full every decision of the courts of last resort in Alabama, Florida, Louisiana, and Mississippi from 1887 to date.

THE SOUTH WESTERN REPORTER. Reports in full every decision of the courts of last resort in Arkansas, Kentucky, Missouri, Tennessee, and Texas from 1886 to date.

THE SUPREME COURT REPORTER. Reports in full every decision of the Supreme Court of the United States from 1882 to date.

SHEPARD'S REPORTER CITATIONS. By the Publisher's Staff, Colorado Springs: Shepard's Citations, Inc.

UNITED STATES REPORTS. The official edition of the reports of the Supreme Court of the United States dating from 1790 with advance sheets to date.

SELECTED BIBLIOGRAPHY

BOOKS

Drury, Robert L., (NOLPE). LAW AND THE SCHOOL SUPERINTENDENT. Cincinnati: The W. H. Anderson Company, 1958.

Edwards, Newton. THE COURTS AND THE PUBLIC SCHOOLS. Chicago: University of Chicago Press, 1955.

Messick, John D. THE DISCRETIONARY POWERS OF SCHOOL BOARDS. Durham, N. C.: Duke University Press, 1949.

Pollack, Ervin H. FUNDAMENTALS OF LEGAL RESEARCH. Brooklyn: The Foundation Press, Inc., 1962.

Price, Miles O. A PRACTICAL MANUAL OF STANDARD LEGAL CITATIONS. New York: Oceana Publications, 1958.

Remmlein, Madeline Kinter. SCHOOL LAW. Danville, Ill.: The Interstate Printers and Publishers, Inc., 1962.

Remmlein, Madeline Kinter and Martha Ware, (NOLPE). AN EVALUATION OF EXISTING FORMS OF SCHOOL LAWS. Cincinnati: The W. H. Anderson Company, 1959.

Seitz, Reynolds C., (NOLPE). LAW AND THE SCHOOL PRINCIPAL. Cincinnati: The W. H. Anderson Company, 1961.

Trusler, Harry Raymond. ESSENTIALS OF SCHOOL LAW. Milwaukee: The Bruce Publishing Company, 1927.

Voorhees, Harvey Cortlandt. THE LAW OF THE PUBLIC SCHOOL SYSTEM OF THE UNITED STATES. Boston: Little, Brown, and Company, 1916.

Weisiger, George B. and Bernita Long Davies. MANUAL FOR THE USE OF LAW BOOKS. Indianapolis: The Bobbs-Merrill Company, Inc., 1961.

FEDERAL GOVERNMENT PUBLICATIONS

United States Bureau of Census. HISTORICAL STATISTICS OF THE UNITED STATES, COLONIAL TIMES TO 1957. Washington, D. C.: United States Government Printing Office, 1960.

United States Bureau of Census. STATISTICAL ABSTRACT OF THE UNITED STATES: 1962. Washington, D. C.: United States Government Printing Office, 1962.

NEWSPAPER ARTICLES

"Teen-Age Clubs in Greensboro Said Drinking and Sex Centers," THE DURHAM SUN (N. C.), LXXIV, No. CXCII (October 10, 1962), 3-A.

"Vandalism Claim Rejected by Court," THE NEWS AND OBSERVER (Raleigh, N. C.), CXCV, No. CXLIV (November 21, 1962), 20.

PERIODICAL ARTICLES

Arnstein, George E. "Students Vote on Student Dress," THE CLEARING HOUSE, XXXII (March, 1958), 387-89.

Bloch, Werner H. "Some Remarks On School Health Examinations," THE JOURNAL OF SCHOOL HEALTH, XXX (November, 1960), 342-46.

Bolmeier, E. C. "Board of Education's Right to Regulate Married Students," JOURNAL OF FAMILY LAW, I (Fall, 1961), 172-80.

Bolmeier, E. C. "The School Principal's Proper Concept of School Law," THE BULLETIN OF THE NATIONAL ASSOCIATION OF SECONDARY-SCHOOL PRINCIPALS, XLII (March, 1958), 1-8.

Bowman, Herman J. "A Review of Discipline," THE BULLETIN OF THE NATIONAL ASSOCIATION OF SECONDARY-SCHOOL PRINCIPALS, XLIII (September, 1959), 147-56.

Burchinal, Lee G. "Do Restrictive Policies Curb Teen Marriages?", OVERVIEW, 1 (March, 1960), 72-73.

Buscher, Velora. "Forsaking All Others," NEA JOURNAL, XLIV (February, 1955), 76-77.

Colmey, James W. and Thomas W. Valentine. "Stop Vandalism with Parent Responsibility Laws," THE AMERICAN SCHOOL BOARD JOURNAL, CXLI (July, 1960), 9-11.

Edwards, Newton. "Stability and Change in Basic Concepts of Law Governing American Education," THE SCHOOL REVIEW, LXV (June, 1957), 161-75.

"Gang Busters," TIME, LIII (January 17, 1949), 46.

Gates, Thomas W. "Passage of the California Anti-Fraternity Statute," California Journal of Education, XXX (February, 1955), 83-88.

Hamilton, Virginia. "Secret Societies in American High Schools," The Bulletin of The National Association of Secondary-School Principals, XL (October, 1956), 22-34.

Handel, Harvey. "Can We Outlaw Fad Clothing?", School Executive, LXXVII (November, 1957), 68-69.

Havinghurst, Robert J. "Early Marriage and the Schools," The School Review, LXIX (Spring, 1961), 36-47.

"High-School Hell," Time, LIV (October 31, 1949), 37.

Kerckhoff, Richard K. and Evelyn Rimel. "Early Marriage, What's All the Fuss About?", The Clearing House, XXXVI (May, 1962), 559-63.

Konold, E. Ewing. "How Can the Administrator Deal With Secret Societies in the Secondary School?", The Bulletin of The National Association of Secondary-School Principals, XXXIV (March, 1950), 278-83.

Landis, Judson T. "Attitudes and Policies Concerning Marriages Among High School Students," Marriage and Family Living, XVIII (May, 1956), 128-36.

"The Legal Status of the Public-School Pupil," National Education Association Research Bulletin, XXVI (February, 1948), 1-39.

Manch, Joseph. "Effective Ways of Regulating Student Dress," The Bulletin of The National Association of Secondary-School Principals, XLI (April, 1957), 144-45.

Matthews, Howard A. "The Courts and Married Students," School Life, XLIV (November-December, 1961), 5-9.

Means, Richard K. "Contributions of the White House Conferences on Children and Youth to School Health Education," The Journal of School Health, XXX (November, 1960), 323-33.

Milligan, John P. and Charles F. Snover. "High School Secret Societies: A Nationwide Problem," American School Board Journal, CXV (August, 1947), 26-28.

Morrison, Gilbert B. "Report of The Committee on Secret Fraternities," JOURNAL OF PROCEEDINGS AND ADDRESSES OF THE FORTY-FOURTH ANNUAL MEETING OF THE NATIONAL EDUCATIONAL ASSOCIATION (July, 1905), 445-51.

Morrison, Gilbert B. "Secret Fraternities in High Schools," JOURNAL OF PROCEEDINGS AND ADDRESSES OF THE FORTY-THIRD ANNUAL MEETING OF THE NATIONAL EDUCATIONAL ASSOCIATION (June, 1904), 484-90.

Probst, Tom. "How To Cut Down Vandalism," THE NATION'S SCHOOLS, LXVIII (September, 1961), 64-68+.

Remmlein, Madeline K. "Can High School Fraternities Exist Legally?", THE BULLETIN OF THE NATIONAL ASSOCIATION OF SECONDARY-SCHOOL PRINCIPALS, XXXI (February, 1947), 55-69.

Rowe, Robert N. "The Legality of Controls Placed On Clothing Worn By Pupils," CALIFORNIA JOURNAL OF SECONDARY EDUCATION, XXXV (January, 1960), 26-30.

"Secret Ceremony," TIME, XLIX (January 13, 1947), 80.

Sperry, Irwin V. and Ruth Thompson. "Marriage Among High School Students," THE BULLETIN OF THE NATIONAL ASSOCIATION OF SECONDARY-SCHOOL PRINCIPLES, XLV (November, 1961), 100-06.

Steinhilber, August W. "Controlling the Use of Student Automobiles," SCHOOL LIFE, XLIV (March, 1962), 23-26.

Strunk, William P. "Exclusion from School as a Disciplinary Tool," THE BULLETIN OF THE NATIONAL ASSOCIATION OF SECONDARY-SCHOOL PRINCIPALS, XLV (October, 1961), 136-44.

Sumption, M. R. "The Control of Pupil Conduct By the School," LAW AND CONTEMPORARY PROBLEMS, XX (Winter, 1959), 80-90.

"Three Cities Move to Toughen Corporal Punishment Policies," NATION'S SCHOOLS, LXXIII (September, 1963), p. 78.

UNPUBLISHED MATERIAL

Brooks, Fred E. "The Legal Status of The Pupil in The American Public Schools, A Study of Common-Law Principles." Unpublished Ph. D. dissertation, University of Chicago, 1948. (Microfilmed.)

Butler, Edward Richard. "Legal Issues Pertaining to The Regulation of Pupil Control In Light of Certain Social Changes 1828 to 1900." Unpublished Ph. D. dissertation, University of Pittsburgh, 1956. (Microfilmed.)

Carroll, L. Gilbert. "The Status of Married Students In the North Carolina Public High Schools." Unpublished Ed. D. dissertation, Duke University, 1960.

Cooper, Louise S. "The Legality and Propriety of Secret Societies In High School." (Unpublished Master's thesis, Department of Education, Duke University, 1959.

Gamberoni, Narcisco Louis. "An Analysis of Appellate Court Decisions Determining The Authority of Boards of Education and Their Agents to Establish Rules and Regulations Governing The Conduct of Pupils, 1900 to 1960." Unpublished Ph. D. dissertation, University of Pittsburgh, 1960.

Johnson, Charles B. "The Legal Status of The Public School Pupil in North Carolina." Unpublished Ed. D. dissertation, Duke University, 1955.

Jones, Roland Walter. "The Legal Rights and Legal Liabilities Involved in Pupil-School Relationships in The Colorado Public Schools." Unpublished Ed. D. dissertation, University of Denver, 1961.

Remaley, J. W. Crane. "The Powers of School Boards in Pupil Exclusion From the Public Schools." Unpublished Ph. D. dissertation, University of Pittsburgh, 1935.

INDEX

References are to section numbers

187

COURTS
Decisions, inconsistency of, 1.2
Responsibility of, 1.2
State
    Alabama, supreme court, 4.2, 4.4, 6.4
    Arizona, supreme court, 5.4, 5.5
    Arkansas, supreme court, 2.4, 4.3, 4.4, 5.2
    California
        District court of appeals, 2.2, 2.4
        Supreme court, 5.2
    Colorado, supreme court, 4.2, 4.4
    Florida, supreme court, 2.2, 2.4
    Georgia
        Superior court of Decatur county, 4.2
        Supreme court, 4.2, 4.3, 4.4
    Illinois, supreme court, 2.4, 5.2
    Indiana
        Supreme court, 2.3, 2.4, 5.2, 6.2
        Tippecanoe circuit court, 2.3
    Iowa, supreme court, 2.2, 4.2, 4.4, 5.3, 5.5, 6.2, 6.3, 6.5
    Kansas, supreme court, 3.3
    Kentucky, court of appeals, 5.2, 6.4
    Louisiana, supreme court, 2.4, 3.2
    Massachusetts, supreme judicial court, 4.3, 4.4, 5.3, 5.4, 6.3
    Michigan, supreme court, 2.2, 2.4, 3.4, 3.5, 5.2, 6.2
    Minnesota, supreme court, 5.4
    Mississippi
        Chancery court of Lafayette county, 2.2
        Supreme court, 2.2, 2.4, 4.2, 4.4
    Missouri, supreme court, 2.4
    Nebraska, supreme court, 6.4
    New Hampshire, supreme court, 5.2
    New York
        Court of appeals, 5.2
        Supreme court of special term, 5.3
        United States district court, 2.4
    North Carolina, supreme court, 2.3, 5.2, 6.2, 6.5
    North Dakota, supreme court, 4.3, 4.4, 5.4
    Ohio
        Common pleas court, 3.3, 3.4, 3.5
        Court of appeals, 2.2, 2.4, 5.3, 5.5
        Supreme court, 3.2, 3.5
    Oklahoma, supreme court, 4.2, 4.4
    Oregon, supreme court, 2.2, 2.4, 5.4
    South Dakota, supreme court, 5.4, 6.2
    Tennessee, supreme court, 3.3, 3.5

INSTITUTIONS — Continued
Oklahoma agricultural and mechanical college, 4.2, 4.4
Palmyra (New Jersey) high school, 6.2
Purdue university, 2.3, 2.4
Seattle high school, 2.3
State industrial school for girls, Alexandria, Louisiana, 3.2
State university of New York, 2.3, 2.4
University of Mississippi, 2.2, 2.4
Wheaton college, 2.3, 2.4
Wilkinson county (Mississippi) agricultural high school, 4.2
JUVENILE DELINQUENCY
Dress associated with, 4.1
Truancy, 3.2
LEGISLATION
Health, 5.2
Parental responsibility, establishing, 6.2, 6.5
Secret societies, prohibiting, 1.3, 2.2, 2.3
LITIGATION
Dress, regulation of
Prescription of certain types, 4.2
Prohibition of certain types, 4.3
Health
Physically and mentally incompetent, attendance of, 5.2
Regulations, enforcement of, 5.2, 5.3, 5.4
Vaccination, a condition for school attendance, 5.2
Legality of school action
Pupil control, methods used in enforcing, 1.4
Reasonableness as a determinant of, 1.2
Marriage, early
Extracurricular activities, exclusion from, 3.4
School attendance regulations, 3.2, 3.3
Misconduct, willful
Public ridicule of school, 6.3
School premises, leaving during school hours, 6.4.
School property, damage to, 6.2
Secret societies
Rules and regulations involving, 2.2, 2.3
Statutes pertaining to, 2.2
MARRIAGE
Attendance
Compulsory, 3.2, 3.5, 7.1
Exclusion from, 3.3, 3.5, 7.1
Freedom from, 3.2, 3.5
Husband, responsibility for wife, 3.2
Right to attend school, 1.3